MW00682155

A Brave, True Story

A Transformational Memoir About
Healing Family Ties and Relationships

NATALIE JOVANIC

Copyright © 2014 by Natalie Jovanic. All rights reserved.
Published by Natalie Jovanic.

No part of this publication may be reproduced, stored in a retrieval
system, or transmitted in any form or by any means, electronic,
mechanical, photocopying, recording, scanning, or otherwise,
without the prior written permission of the publisher.

Library and Archives Canada Cataloguing in Publication

Jovanic, Natalie, 1973–, author
    A brave true story: a transformational memoir on healing
family ties and relationships / Natalie Jovanic ; [edited by] Kathy Kaiser.

Includes bibliographical references.

ISBN 978-0-9911330-0-0 (pbk.)

1. Jovanic, Natalie, 1973– —Childhood and youth. 2. Jovanic,
Natalie, 1973– —Relations with men. 3. Family counselors—
Biography. 4. Abused women—Biography. 5. Adult child sexual
abuse victims—Biography. I. Kaiser, Kathy, 1954–, editor II. Title.

HV697.J69 2014   362.82'86   C2013-907502–X

Cover and book design by the Vancouver Desktop Publishing Centre
Copyediting by Kathy Kaiser
Author photograph copyright © 2013 by Katherin Wermke

Thank you for your support!

You help me to support the non-profit association "Streets Heroes of India (SOI)" with a percentage of the sales profit of this book and I am very grateful for your help.

SOI is an international association of professionals that offers training, counseling and support for the care staff of care centers and orphanages for emotional and psychosocial rehabilitation of children and youth in India. They also work with Indian children and young people from very traumatic scenarios to develop and apply all their potential and skill so that they can reestablish their purpose in life, becoming productive and responsible citizens throughout their life. I invite you to follow their page on facebook under **SOI, Street-Heroes Of India.**

To my sister
I love you

Contents

Foreword   9

Preface and Disclaimer   11

Part One: Conflict and Adaptation

Introduction   15

My Early Life   17

My Father's World   19

Two Worlds Collide   26

My Mother's World   31

The Final Curtain   40

Part Two: The Show Must Go On

Ignoring My Inner Voice   49

Yearning for Love   68

Facing Reality   81

Every End Is a New Beginning   100

Too Afraid to Look   109

Tell Me, Where Have Our Dreams Gone?   113

Swimming in the Vortex of Change   133

Part Three: True Healing

I Fulfill My Yearning for Love   157

I Transform My Story   178

Invisible Energies   190

Integrating Two Worlds   202

A Relationship Is a Dance of Two   208

My Magical Story   227

Especially for You   230

Bibliography of Further Reading   234

Acknowledgments   236

About the Author   238

Foreword

From the beginning of time, we have been telling stories. Every culture, every language, every race; we all tell stories. Through the ages, storytelling is the way that we preserve our history and culture, record our experience and illustrate our values. We come alive when we tell stories. And we understand our place in the world by the stories that we are told.

Storytelling, in its essence, allows healing. It creates a safe space where the wounded experience can be remembered, breathed, heard, and often exorcised.

So often the stories that need the most healing are left untold. The presence of blame, shame and fear can stop us from having access to this natural healing process, the telling of the story.

Throughout the years of sharing stories, both the telling and the listening, I have come to recognize the transformation that people undergo simply by being present to story. By sharing a story of a traumatic experience we realize that we are not alone. The telling and the listening are of equal value.

There is a magical triangle that I imagine floating through the air, like a bubble with moving, shifting angles. The corners of this triangle are made of three components; the storyteller, the story-listener and the story. None of the three can exist without the other.

The walls of this triangle are malleable; the nature of each component is always slightly different for each telling of the story. The precious space that lives within the three elements, I've come to believe, is courage.

It requires a huge amount of courage to dive into the story space where trauma and abuse is remembered. The voices of criticism, blame and judgment, both internal and external, are powerful enough to quieten these stories, sometimes for life. And yet, telling these crucial stories can be a matter of living or simply doing the motions of life.

I have been honored to witness the bravery of people willing to finally tell their stories. It is always a moment of immense courage. It is sometimes overwhelming. It is awesome and a great privilege.

A Brave True Story is exactly that; the courage to express the story that reaches out to meet the experience of so many others who have lived through abuse, fear and enormous pain. It is an important story. One that needs to be witnessed, truly heard and told out loud without shame, without pain but with the pride that goes far beyond survival to a place of inspiring empowerment.

Lisa Bloom
Founder of Story Coach
Author of the Amazon Bestseller 'Cinderella and the Coach–
the Power of Storytelling for Coaching Success'
www.story-coach.com

Preface and Disclaimer

This is my story and I've told it, as I remember it, to the best of my ability. The story is my truth, but I know that I am the only one who sees the world through my eyes. I can't decide what is true for others in a larger sense, and I do not wish to argue or change their truth or their reality. My intent in telling my story is not to blame anyone or seek justice. I'm telling it because I believe my story can help others identify areas in their own lives that require healing. I'm telling it so that others can learn about healing techniques and start their own healing process. I'm telling it to give others hope. Healing is possible. Having a healthy relationship is possible.

A few more words about my story: It is a memoir, a work of creative nonfiction. The events I share are portrayed to the best of my memory. But it is not a word-for-word transcript or a comprehensive report of all that has happened to me. Some names, places, and identifying details have been changed to protect the privacy of the people involved. In some places, I have changed or added details to help move the story along. That said, everything in this book is consistent with the truth of what I experienced.

—*Natalie Jovanic*

PART ONE
Conflict and Adaptation

Introduction

In August 2013, I went to India to present my workshop, "Storytelling: How the Magical World of Stories Can Heal Trauma and Violence," to counselors.

The counselors there worked for Don Bosco, a Roman Catholic institute that was responsible for orphanages whose residents often had suffered violence and abuse.

During the workshop, I shared my knowledge about the therapeutic power of stories. For me, each story has its beauty, and we counselors and coaches should help our clients recognize the beauty in their own stories. Each story is a raw diamond, and we have to support our clients in polishing it so that its brilliance shows.

At the end of the two-day workshop, one of the counselors, a nun in a salmon-colored sari, asked for the microphone. She stood in front of the group and read a speech expressing gratitude for what I had taught them. While she spoke, I looked at the group of mostly women, many in colorful saris. In some of their eyes, I could see that they had found diamonds in the stories they had shared during the workshop. Moved by their gratitude, tears sprang to my eyes. When she returned the microphone, I said, "I taught you what I believe in."

It was true that I had passed on to them what I believed in, but it wasn't just knowledge, theory, and professional experience. I had taught them what had helped me heal from sexual and emotional violence, rejection, and conflict and what had helped me clear out the abusive relationship patterns I had learned as a child. My journey to well-being took me about eighteen years, and because of it, I experienced inner changes that earlier I would not have believed possible.

I share my story in this book because I believe it can help you do the following:

- Identify areas in your own life that may require healing.
- Learn the differences between an abusive relationship and a healthy relationship.
- Find out about different healing techniques.
- Start your own healing process and find the beauty in your story.
- See that despite your situation right now, there is always hope. Healing is possible. Having a healthy relationship is possible.

My Early Life

The first event that I remember occurred when I was three years old. That day, I was in a room where thin daylight entered through the window at the end of the room. On one wall, there was a shelf. Another wall had a crib attached to it. I sat in the middle of the room on the floor. At three, I had big brown eyes and short brown hair. My body was plump. An observer might not have been able to guess whether I was a girl or a boy. My short little arms held some colorful toy blocks, which I moved around joyfully. I was concentrating deeply on my task of creating an imaginary world. I enjoyed my play alone.

Behind my back, the door opened. A man hidden by the darkness of the hallway entered the room, sneaking in like a thief. He was tall and dark. I was so deeply involved in my play that I didn't notice him at first. The man approached me slowly, step by quiet step. Suddenly, I noticed his presence. I turned around and saw the man but could not see his face. I smiled and held my little arms out to him. I knew him and I was happy to see him. I did not yet know what would happen. I trusted him. I was innocent and I had dignity, though I was just a little child.

The man opened his trousers and did what he wanted to do. After he was done, he left the room.

I became a little body without movement. My arms and legs were stretched out on the floor, and my face had lost its smile. I felt dirty. It was a kind of dirt that would not wash away with water. The sun had gone. The colors had gone. The warmth had gone. Cold, black darkness surrounded me.

That day, a part of me died. There was no longer any carefree play; there was no longer any lighthearted fun. My innocence was gone. I lost my connection to the world and to other people. I withdrew into my own inner world, a lonely and empty place.

The pain that I felt that day was too much for me. I cut my connection with the outside world and constructed thick, invisible walls around myself. The walls protected me from feeling further pain—and prevented me from deeply connecting with other people. My life continued and I grew up with this secret in my heart. The burden of it was heavy, too heavy to share with another person.

My Father's World

It was the first Saturday of April in 1979. I was six years old, and I was sitting at the counter in our kitchen, where we usually had breakfast and lunch, and staring at the mirror in front of me. The mirror was decorated with an elegant Frenchwoman wearing a costume from the early twentieth century. I noticed my reflection, a girl with dark brown eyes and a plump body. How ugly I was. I would never be as elegant and feminine as the woman on the mirror.

It was already 9:10 a.m. He was late again. When would he come this time? The bell at the entrance gate rang, and the sound made me wince. I hated it when he was late, maybe because I silently hoped that he had forgotten. I breathed deeply. There was no escape. It was time to leave my mother's house, where I lived with her, my stepfather, Wolfgang, and my nine-year-old sister, Anna, and visit my father for the weekend. The court had given him visitation rights for my sister and me for one weekend each month, two weeks in August, and one week during the Christmas holiday. I went into the corridor and got my bag. Mami waited there to give my sister and me a farewell kiss.

Together, Anna and I walked down the long corridor toward the door and stepped out to the pathway that led from the house to the street. We turned right and passed by the flower bed and the fence to our garden. Some daffodils and tulips were in bloom, and the bushes behind the fence had started to show their first green buds. We passed by the car park, where the new silver-green BMW of my stepfather and the old red VW of our disabled neighbor were parked. The VW owner lived with her mother in an old house close to the street. Their garden was full of beech trees with massive trunks and an oak tree. We passed by their door, and I saw Papa waiting in front of the closed gate. He was a tall, strong man with glasses. He had a moustache, dark hair, and blue eyes, and he had a big, round head.

I would enter into another world now, one where I had to comply with my father's rules. I opened the gate and greeted him.

He gave me a kiss. His moustache scratched my skin, and I felt heaviness in his embrace. He drove his old white BMW toward his apartment in an anonymous apartment complex in a suburb of Munich.

Thirty minutes later, he opened the door to his apartment, which was on the third floor. To the left side was his bedroom. We slept there in the same bed with him when he did not have a girlfriend. If he had a girlfriend, we were allowed to use other mattresses. Opposite the entrance door was the bathroom; to the right side was the living room.

After leaving our bags in the bedroom, my sister and I helped him sort his dirty clothes in the bathroom. Somehow, Papa always managed to do this task while we were there. So I sorted his dirty underwear and towels, as well as his shirts, T-shirts, and trousers.

At dinner, Anna and I sat at his white kitchen table. The kitchen had a balcony and a huge window. He lit a candle and prepared *eierbrote*, which was bread soaked in egg and then fried. He put a piece on my plate. I poured a lot of ketchup on top and chewed with pleasure. I concentrated on the meal and forgot everything around me.

On Sunday, we got up late and had breakfast, starting with bread and strawberry jam. He was standing in front of the stove to prepare some boiled eggs when he said, "I don't know what this Schmidt and your mother are thinking. Children shouldn't be told that their mother has a fatal illness."

He never called Wolfgang by his first name. This felt like

an insult. I concentrated on the bread in front of me while his words put sadness in my heart. At my mother's house, we never spoke about her illness. She vanished into the hospital once in a while, and my grandmother took care of us. Every time she came back, her face had changed. Papa's words always struck fear into me. I didn't necessarily know what they meant, but they always seemed horrible. I decided to put more strawberry jam on the bread, so that the layer of jam was thicker than the bread, and chewed my bread and jam thoroughly. The taste of the jam relaxed me, but I just wanted to go home. I would have to wait another six hours. Later, Anna and I helped our father clean his apartment.

I looked at the clock: 5:00 p.m. We should be at home at 6:00 p.m. We needed about half an hour to get there. I was nervous. Would we arrive punctually this time? Normally, he'd return us late.

Then he said in a depressed voice, "Let's sit down on the sofa before I take you home." He pointed at the worn-out beige leather sofa in front of the window. My mood lowered. I knew what would follow. Just another time that we would arrive home late. What would Mami think about this? She would be waiting for us.

Papa went to the stereo and looked for an album. A few seconds later, the room was filled with Beethoven. How I hated that music! It was so sad. Papa returned to the sofa and sat down. He gestured to us and I followed him and lay down by his right side, with my head resting on his lower belly and his legs. My sister sat by his left side. His hand lay on my shoulder. The masculine smell of his trousers—some combination of urine and sweat and musk—entered my nose as I lay there. It was such a well-known smell. *Will I ever in my life forget this smell?* I asked myself. Then he started with his usual words, "Your mother was so mean to me when she separated us. She and her family have taken away everything I had."

Tears coursed down his face and his body shook. I was miserable lying there because my father seemed so gloomy and rejected. After about an hour, he got up. "I need to show you something." Anna and I rose and followed him.

We got into his car and drove to a little chapel close to where my mother lived. He slowly strolled down the hall of the cloister, pausing in front of each Station of the Cross and looking at each sculpture. My sister and I followed him silently and at a distance. I felt so uneasy. I hated churches. I was anxious to get back home to Mami.

This became his routine. Every time we visited him for the following four years, he would cry, and then we would make the trip to the chapel.

My father was born in Munich, Germany, at the beginning of World War II. He was the third child out of four. His father, my grandfather, came from Croatia, and I imagine that their lives were dictated by fear and worries during the Third Reich because they were foreigners. When my father was nineteen, my grandfather put a noose around a doorknob in their apartment, put his neck in the noose, and sat down, thus strangling himself. My father found the body. My mother was the one to tell me this story; my father never talked about it. She also told me that when my father was young, he swam and played the saxophone and the flute.

When I was one year old, my father found my mother in bed with a friend, Wolfgang. After that, my mother left my father and moved in with her parents. Later, she married Wolfgang, who had left his wife and two daughters.

My father never forgave my mother. He would point out to my sister and me that he was a Catholic, and so for him, marriage lasted until death. In hindsight, I realize that my father called himself a Catholic only when it suited him. For example, I don't remember that he ever went to church. And I recall that he lived with a few girlfriends without getting married.

When I was young, my father suspected that I wasn't his daughter but Wolfgang's. When I grew up, my physical features proved that I was in fact his daughter.

When my parents separated, I did not see my father again until I was three years old. In this period, my father wasn't interested in seeing me, only my older sister. My relationship with my father was difficult. When I was five, I locked myself in the bathroom, crying because I didn't want to see him. My mother had to coax me out and then push me out of the house to see him. Later, I would escape into illness to avoid having to visit him. Otitis, an inflammation of the ear, was my body's method of protecting myself. I was afraid of my father and rejected him. Yet there was also another side to our relationship.

About two years after my father first visited the chapel with Anna and me, my sister and I arrived at his apartment on another Saturday morning. In his bedroom, I prepared the blankets for the two mattresses that lay in front of the orange-curtained windows. Over the past few years, Anna and I had grown more and more unwilling to sleep in the same bed with him; finally, the court had forced him to allow us to use our own mattresses even if he did not have a girlfriend in bed with him.

My father came into the room with his usual ponderous steps, the corners of his mouth turned down. He said, "You do not have to do this. We will visit your aunt in Neunburg."

I looked at the blankets in my hands. In Neunburg, Anna and I had to sleep in the same bed that he did—my aunt didn't have a separate room for us. It was a small room with a double bed, and the pitch of the roof made the ceiling so low it seemed that it would press you down to the floor. In my mind's eye, I saw the bed with Papa, Anna, and me lying in it. He lay on his back in a beige undershirt, snoring like always. The smell of his armpit came into my nose. I didn't want to sleep in the same bed with him. Tears welled up in my eyes. My whole body contracted. I tried to swallow the tears. Too late. The first tear ran down my face. My stomach cramped so strongly that I had to clasp it. Inside, there was a voice yearning for my mother. *Please help me, Mami. I don't want to visit my aunt. I want to go home to you. I want to be safe. The other part said firmly, But you are used to sleeping in the same bed with him. That is normal. It does not harm you. You will hurt his feelings if you complain.*

When Papa saw my tears, he came over and hugged me. His hugs were always unpleasant. I wanted to be hugged by Mami instead. I wanted to push him away. Yet I didn't. He asked, "What's wrong?" Should I tell him the truth? No, I couldn't. It would hurt him. He already was such a sad man. He had suffered so much due to the divorce. I couldn't tell him that I didn't want to be with him, that I didn't want to sleep in the same bed with him. "I just have a stomachache. I don't know why. It is just hurting so much." He hugged me again and then turned around to pack his bag.

An hour later, we all sat in his new red sports car. I sat in the back and sang, "My Bonnie lies over the ocean, / my Bonnie lies over the sea . . . / O bring back my Bonnie to me."

I sang wholeheartedly, although each note was wrong, and I felt some sort of comfort and peace for the moment.

Hidden behind all my fears of and rejection of my father, I loved him as he was. I wanted to see him happy, and I did everything I could to make him happy. I didn't know about boundaries or where to put them. I was a loyal child, driven by a blind and innocent love. I had no idea how to distinguish between right and wrong, good and bad. I yearned to receive his love, and this made me adapt until I abandoned myself, disrespecting my own needs and limits.

My sister and I continued to visit our father regularly for years. He always picked us up a little late and drove us to his apartment. He continued to insult our mother's family and Wolfgang. I can't remember that he ever said a conciliatory word about them. My maternal grandmother died when I was ten years old, and after her death, my father's continual bad-mouthing of my mother's family became too much.

Due to the fact that we also had more stress in school, Anna finally asked him whether we could visit him during the day once a month instead of staying overnight. Anna was the child my father had wanted. While I had withdrawn internally, never saying a word, my sister was a fighter and communicated her needs.

When she made her request, our father sat down in the living room with us and explained that, according to Freud, we were acting from the superego, which was represented by our mother. He explained Freud's theory further, with more details about how we had been influenced by our mother, and he added something about the id and the ego. I didn't understand much of what he said, but it made me feel uncomfortable and pressured.

Finally, he said that we had to decide: either we would visit once a month and stay overnight or not visit him ever again. We decided not to visit our father again.

He continued to send us letters and postcards. When he sent me birthday wishes, he regularly did so either on the wrong day or for the wrong age. When I was sixteen, he married an Italian woman, Gabriela.

Two Worlds Collide

I can't remember anything about the time when my parents lived together, because they separated when I was one year old. In my entire life, I can remember seeing my parents together only twice.

One of these days was a Saturday, when Anna and I were visiting our father. After we had arrived at his apartment, he suddenly announced, "Let's go hiking in the mountains!"

My heart was jubilant. Finally, I could get outside, not be locked up in the apartment with him. Being in nature was always a relief for me, a little bit of light in the darkness.

"Yes! I want to go! But I do not have my hiking boots with me!" I said.

"We'll return to your mother's house and ask for the hiking boots," he replied.

Return to my mother's place with him? I could not remember having ever seen my parents talk with each other. I looked at my sister. She didn't react.

Go with him now to Mami's place? It did not feel right. What would Mami feel when she saw me with him at my side? Suddenly, my eagerness to go hiking disappeared, and my heart grew heavy. What would Mami think? My mother was very distant from my father. I believed that she would have preferred to cut him out of her life completely, because she did not know how to deal with him. Maybe the idea was not so good.

It was too late. Our father drove us to our mother's house, passing by the huge forest. I stared out the window, seeing the darkness of the trees. The forest seemed impenetrable. To calm myself, I tried to count the trunks of the fir trees. Finally, we arrived at the wooden gate. My father opened the gate triumphantly and strode down the path for the first time in his life. He held us by our hands, Anna on his right side and me on his left. His grip was firm. Had I given him an excuse to invade Mami's house? I felt guilty. I could not stop him. He rang the bell, stepped back, and waited.

Mami opened the door. I saw a vulnerable woman, her face marked by the scars from the operations on her face for cancer. Never before had I seen my mother from this perspective. I would have loved to run to her and hug her, but I was not allowed to, because it was Papa's weekend. Papa never allowed me to love Mami. I always felt that he expected me to love only him. I knew how to separate my two worlds. I'd never do something that would hurt him during my visits. I wasn't allowed to love Mami or say anything positive about Mami's family when I stayed with him. He rejected her. When I was with my mother, my father became rejected and the outcast. Sometimes, I felt that the only reason my mother allowed me to have contact with him was the law. This was his right. But other times, my mother made it clear that it was a good thing for me to have a relationship with my father.

Now my father said, "I want to go hiking with my daughters. Give me their hiking boots."

My mother looked at him with her huge green eyes, which transmitted a special sadness at that moment. "I will not allow you to go hiking with the girls. You know what happened last year."

The year before, we had hiked with our father in the Dolomites and been surprised by a thunderstorm with hail and intense rain. The mountain had become black and dangerous. Soaked to the skin, we had reached a hut. But Papa had refused to stay in the hut overnight because he did not have his toothbrush with him, and he had forced us out again into the rain while darkness started to fall. We had crossed a windy valley, full of stones and debris, and made our descent through the woods, more slipping than walking. We had made it back to our tent at midnight.

Now Papa grew angry and raised his voice: "You can't deprive me of the hiking boots. I have a right to take them!"

Mami's coloring seemed to change to pale gray, transforming her into a fragile porcelain doll. I stood at Papa's side while my two worlds collided. I shifted from one foot to the other. How I longed to help Mami—she seemed so far away and unreachable. What would she think of me? What would happen when I returned on Sunday? I had brought him to her house. I withdrew into my inner world, trying to be invisible. Sometimes it was better not to be seen. The discussion continued for twenty minutes, until Mami reentered the house and closed the door. Papa withdrew reluctantly, without the hiking boots.

My parents met during Carnival, an exuberantly festive event before Lent. My mother was eighteen and my father was two years older. Papa was Mami's first boyfriend. When my mother was nineteen, she got pregnant. My grandfather went with her to Holland to have an abortion. I don't know how my father felt about this, but I assume that he disapproved of it. Mami once told Anna that the abortion had welded them together. Papa never talked about the abortion.

Later, they got married and my sister was born. My mother was an only child and wanted to have another one. When my father refused, she betrayed him—she secretly stopped taking the Pill and became pregnant with me.

Three months prior to my birth, she and my father both signed a paper titled "My Obligations as a Good Wife." I found it many years later in a storage room. It laid out the rules of the household. Some examples: "It is my obligation to kiss my husband in the morning and when he returns home." "I have to hug my husband if he wants me to." "My husband has the right to go out alone."

How would my mother have felt signing such a paper? After my birth, she cheated on my father with Wolfgang. When my father found the two of them together, she moved to her parents' house.

The separation was the beginning of a never-ending war. Two people used their children to fight with each other, two people who may have felt love for each other once but who now felt only hatred. My father saw my mother as the source of all evil, and he accepted a divorce only when the German government decided to change the law and eliminate the option of a guilty party to a divorce. My father insisted that my mother had stuck her tongue out at him when she left court, after having received custody of my sister and me. My mother repeated stories about her helplessness in the face of my father's hostility. How could she deal with this vindictive man? She would never be able to get rid of him, she said. And she was right. At least once a year, they met in court to argue about child support or visitation rights. Both of them continued telling their stories, year after year. There was no change, there was no forgiveness, no healing of the wounds.

Some years later, when I was fifteen, my mother, my sister, and I went skiing in Lermoos, a village in Tyrol about an hour's drive from Munich.

We stood together at the edge of the slope, about to take the last descent before going home. Suddenly, I saw a figure on the ski slope above us. The upper part of his body was bent forward, and he wore a light blue overall. I knew this man's skiing style—it was my father. My body went rigid. What would happen if he saw us? In the same moment, I pitied him. I wanted to run to him and hug him. He seemed so alone. As he came closer, he recognized us and approached us. For a moment, he looked into my mother's eyes. I felt her discomfort. He said, "Nice to see you." His tone was sarcastic and he stared at the scars on my mother's face. My mother looked at Anna and me and said, "If you want, you can go downhill with him. I'll wait for you here until you return." We nodded. When I left, I saw the slender, frail figure of my mother at the edge of the slope, waiting for us.

When I was with my father, it seemed to mean that I was rejecting my mother—and the other way around. To adapt to these two different worlds, I put on one mask in my mother's world and another in my father's world. I knew what I had to say to please the parent in each world.

Inside me, the demands of these two worlds collided constantly. In a way, these worlds were opposites: one was force and one was vulnerability. But they were alike in their hatred of each other. Who was I? I did not know. I constructed lies so that I wouldn't hurt either parent. This was the conflict I lived with—constantly rejecting the part of myself that wanted to be authentic and speak honestly.

My Mother's World

After my parents' separation, my sister and I lived with my mother. When I was three, my mother was diagnosed with a rare form of cancer that affected the glands in her face. My mother was a beautiful woman in her thirties, and in the first surgery the doctors took care not to scar her face. The cancer returned twice during the following three years. The second and third times, she stayed in the hospital for a long time, and when she returned, her face had changed.

It was in the summer of 1979 that my mother underwent a third cancer surgery on her face. The surgery was split into two parts: the first part consisted of removing the cancerous tissue on the left part of her face; later, the doctors would transplant skin from her shoulder to her left cheek.

When Mami had just returned home after the first part of the surgery, we all sat together at our dining table. In the fireplace in the left corner of the room, steaks and vegetables sizzled on a grill above gleaming red charcoal. The window on the other side of the room opened to the garden, which became a green jungle during summertime. Anna sat to my right on a huge chair covered with a violet-brown cloth that was decorated with small pink and blue flowers. Wolfgang and Mami sat opposite us on the sofa, which was covered in the same material. The brown marble table was covered with all the ingredients of a barbecue: a selection of sauces, bread, and a bowl with all the food that was already cooked. The left side of my mother's face was covered with a white bandage. She started to eat her steak. I sat in my chair, my eyes glued to my plate, which was filled with sausages, a huge baked potato, and tons of ketchup. I didn't dare look up. What if the meat dissolved the bandage? What if it fell off, and I had to see all the way through to her teeth? I halfheartedly chewed on my meat. It didn't taste very good. I could hardly swallow. I didn't want to eat with her. Nervously, I glanced at Mami. What would I see? Would the bandage be soaked with blood? Or pus? The clean, white bandage was still in place, but my fear that it might dissolve remained. My own mother had turned into a monster. I was in a horror show.

After some days, my sister and I went to visit my father for our summer holiday. It was a relief that I didn't have to see my mother's face during that time. After two weeks, we returned. The next morning, Anna and I went into the attic to look for something. Suddenly, we found a new photo. It showed my mother in her bikini in our garden. She sat relaxed on the garden chair. Then I looked at her face. On the right side, there was a cheek. On the left side, there was a hole exposing her teeth; her head was just a skull. I saw a real monster.

When I grew older, I got used to my mother's face. I do not have any memories of her face before the surgeries except from photos. People stared at her everywhere—on the train, in shops, and on the road. It must have been a difficult experience for her, yet she never talked about it. When I stood by her side on the train, I always wanted to protect her from the horrified looks of other people. From my child's perspective, she was the most beautiful woman on Earth.

My mother was born during World War II in Brandenburg. She was the only surviving child of my grandparents. Her older brother had died being born. During the war, the family moved to Berlin. They had been bombed several times and had lost everything during the bombings; they must have spent countless nights in the bunkers.

After the war, when my mother was about four, my grandfather became a prisoner of war of the Soviet Union. He had not served in the German armed forces but had been the chief executive officer of a printing company in Berlin. When the Soviets invaded Berlin, he was put in prison due to his important position in the company. My grandmother and my mother lived in Germany after the war and managed to flee from what had become East Berlin to Munich, West Germany. After seven years, my grandfather came back from captivity and reunited with his family. I don't know any details beyond this, but I know that they all must have experienced extreme trauma during the war and during the postwar era.

In my early childhood, my relationship with my mother was affected by our separations while she was in the hospital. Her capacity to give love during this time was limited, because she was struggling to survive. I didn't experience stability or security in our relationship. We became closer when I was seven, after my mother found out for the first time that Wolfgang had cheated on her. She even found photos of his naked girlfriend in his home office, where he had left them on the table.

Wolfgang's great passion, or maybe addiction, was to photograph or film everything. He took photos of my mother while she was lying in intensive care after her surgeries. During our holidays, he photographed our plates filled with food; we couldn't eat until he had taken his pictures.

If his eyes were not hidden by the camera, it usually meant that he was offended by something that my sister or I had done. It was not always clear what it was, but we would know that he was in a bad mood. He made sure that we felt his suffering. Sometimes, he would explode and hit either my sister or me.

Wolfgang had a peculiar phobia: a fear of air-conditioning or of any breeze that was produced by open car windows. When we went for holidays in France, we all sat in a hot car because the windows had to be closed and the air-conditioning turned off. If we sat near the air conditioner in a restaurant, he would complain bitterly and make us change seats. I never saw him really ill, but a breeze of any sort seemed to produce great suffering in him—or maybe that was just what he wanted us to believe. I often wondered if this fear was actually Wolfgang's way of getting attention and imposing his will on the rest of his family.

After his infidelity, my mother stayed with Wolfgang. I noticed that she started to wear makeup again. And she also returned to teaching full time at the local gymnasium, a German school that prepares students for university. Later, my mother caught Wolfgang cheating again. Still, she stayed with him.

My stepfather had another odd habit: he insisted that he be the one to pick up the mail from our mailbox. I didn't understand this quirk of his until years later, when my maternal grandfather told me that while we were on holidays, he used to throw away postcards sent to my stepfather. Wolfgang was a sales representative, and during the week he ate his lunch in restaurants all over Munich. The postcards were from waitresses. My grandfather didn't want my mother to know the truth. I believe that he thought that he was doing his best to hold his daughter's marriage together. Perhaps it was because of my stepfather's betrayals that my mother used to say that my sister and I were the most important people in her life and that we were her reason for living.

After the third surgery, the cancer did not return—for a while. But my mother never believed that she would grow old. And I had a gnawing sense that I would lose her early. There was no hope that a healing would be possible. The return of the cancer seemed to be as sure as the explosion of a ticking time bomb.

When I was ten, I started attending the same school where Mami taught economics, law, and geography. Once she said to the mother of a friend of mine, who was her student, "I would be happy to live to see my younger daughter complete her school-leaving exam." This belief would shape her destiny.

Ten years after my mother's third surgery, when I was sixteen, her cancer returned with metastases in the lungs and esophagus, both inoperable. Death was only a matter of time. My sister and I took care of my mother while my stepfather worked. My sister went with her on countless hospital visits. My mother started chemotherapy and then stopped. She went to a psychological support group once and then quit. A colleague gave her some esoteric and spiritual books as a present, but my mother refused to read them. Instead, I read them.

Each day, she and I would walk our dog, Mimic, in the forest. I wanted to spend every possible moment with her. With each passing month, my mother lost a bit more vitality.

Two years later, the cancer had progressed so much that my mother had lost most of her ability to swallow. When I looked at her, I could see that she was dying, and I didn't know how to deal with it. My mother and sister were the only people I could rely on. I had never regarded my father, Wolfgang, or my grandfather in that light. Other cherished companions in my life were our two cats, Charly and Chloe, and our dog, Mimic.

Many nights, I lay in my bed crying. One night in May of 1991, I woke up because my stomach hurt terribly. I wasn't able to move. I didn't know what to do. I didn't want to bother my mother, because she was already fighting terminal cancer. I didn't want to worry her even more, yet the pain became unbearable. I wasn't able to move. I screamed for my Mami.

She came into my room, thin and weak, and asked me, "What is going on?" I replied that I had terrible stomach cramps. She took me to the emergency room. I spent the night there in a dark basement room. The next morning, several doctors examined me but could find nothing. In the afternoon, my mother came to pick me up. We sat down in the doctor's office to have a conversation with Laura, the emergency room doctor. She looked at my mother and at me and said, "We examined your daughter and ran several tests. We haven't found anything. Taking into

account your illness, we assume that the pain is psychosomatic."
She looked into my mother's eyes and continued, "I am train-
ing to become a psychologist. I could have a session with your
daughter to help her through this situation. What do you think?"
My mother looked at me. I nodded shyly and she replied, "OK,
Natalie will have a session with you."

One week later, I entered Laura's apartment, which was in an
old, modest four-story apartment house in the heart of Munich;
it was part of a homogeneous complex of beige buildings, each
one just like the other. I sat on the green sofa in her living room.
The room was serene except for the noise of car engines when
the traffic lights turned green on the busy street. The blinds
were down to keep out the heat of the afternoon sun. An elegant
old wooden table with four chairs stood in front of the window.
A bookshelf loaded with books was on one side of the room.
I could not make out any of the titles amid the clutter. What
would happen now?

Laura sat opposite me. She was a tall woman with blonde hair
and a gentle, warm smile. I took a breath. What did she want me
to tell her? I had never visited a psychologist before, nor was I
used to talking about myself. Nobody had ever asked me how
I felt about my mother's impending death. What should I talk
about? My agony seeing that my Mami swallowed less and less
every day and had to vomit up all that could not go into her
stomach because of the tumor in her esophagus? All the nights
that I lay in my bed, my pillow wet with tears, begging God
to let me die instead of her? That my stepfather was rarely at
home, and my sister and I took care of Mami? That I knew that
he would hit me if I did not do what he expected? That I loved
those precious moments when I went for a walk with Mami and
our dog in the forest? I stayed silent and looked at her.

"Tell me something about your family," Laura said. *My family.* Suddenly, an inner dam broke and I burst into tears. I could
not stop crying. "Papa, you know, it is so horrible with Papa," I

gasped. The shadow of my father rose in front of me, growing bigger and bigger, almighty and powerful. It occupied the entire room. I sat opposite him on the sofa and felt like a little mouse threatened by a cobra that stood there with an erect neck and venom-spreading teeth. Horrified by my own inevitable death, I felt powerless to escape him. The shadow wrapped itself around me. Crying, I looked at Laura, desperately longing for a hug to feel a bit of connection and a bit of comfort for my pain. My mind told me, *Are you crazy? You are supposed to talk about your mother. She is the one who will die. Why do you cry about Papa?* I heard my mother's voice in my head: *You have to accept him as he is.*

I could not stop crying and was unable to speak. Laura just looked at me. At the end of our session, she got up from her chair, accompanied me to the door, and said, "I think it would be good if we worked together. It could be really helpful for you. Think about it." She smiled encouragingly.

I nodded automatically. "OK. Thank you. Good-bye." I ran down the staircase, still horrified by the shadow I had met in Laura's living room. My mother was waiting for me in the car.

"How was it?"

I could not share my experience. I was too afraid of it. "Well, it was OK. But I don't think that it will be useful for me. I don't want to go back."

"OK. It was worth a try."

I nodded and took a breath. I stared out the window. I did not want to show her my terror.

My mother always said that my father would be my only remaining parent after her death and that I should keep in touch with him because she wanted me to have a dad. Maybe she thought that when I got older, my relationship with my father would improve. At any rate, I did not want her to worry. I wanted her to die peacefully. I sat next to her and tried to calm the giant waves of emotion that washed over my body. He was my father, the only one I had.

Some months later, the doctors told my mother to stop eating meat; it was too difficult for her to digest it. I took this opportunity to become a vegetarian in solidarity with my mother. I had stopped eating rabbit after we had our first rabbit as a pet when I was ten. Over the years, I had grown to dislike eating meat, even though we ate a lot of it at home. I never would have been able to kill an animal, so it didn't feel right to eat an animal. Naturally, my mother hated having to avoid meat: it was a sign that her body was decaying.

The months passed and my mother completely lost her ability to eat; she had to get her nutrition from a stomach tube. She didn't want to die in a hospital, so her bedroom was converted into an intensive care unit. On Christmas of 1991, she had to start taking morphine for pain.

Nine months later, on a warm evening in September 1992, I entered my mother's bedroom. I was alone with her. The blinds were partly down to prevent the sun from entering the room. At her side were a bedpan and an oxygen cylinder to help her breathe when she suffered from shortness of breath. My mother was lying on the bed, her skin pale, her eyes closed. Next to her face was the bucket where she would spit her saliva because she wasn't able to swallow anymore. The room smelled clinical.

I sat down by her side. It was time to feed her through the stomach tube. I tenderly touched her arm to wake her up. She opened her eyes and looked at me. I tried to smile. Then she said, "Natalie, there is one thing I have to tell you. The only person who has failed in this situation is you." Her tone was cold. Had she really said that? I couldn't believe her words. I hoped that I had misunderstood. I was shocked. I loved her so much. She had told me that I had failed. I didn't understand. I wanted to clarify or just to understand. She pushed my arm away and made a sign that I should leave the room. She meant what she had said. I left, my heart broken. I didn't know what to do anymore. It was the last time that my mother and I spoke.

How had I failed? My mother, I believe, must have been

referring to her imminent death. Like my stepfather and even my grandfather, she must have thought that my demands on her could make her cancer return. More, she must have thought that I did make her cancer return.

My mother's rejection produced deep feelings of guilt and shame in me. For many years, I believed her words. They left a deep wound in my heart. It took me years until I was able to talk about it, because I was convinced that her words were true and that I had failed.

My mother's death was cruel and devastating. She wasn't able to let go of life, and she was horribly afraid of dying. On my good days, my explanation to myself was that she said it because she was bitter about the fact that she would die soon while I would continue living. Also, she had been under the influence of morphine for nine months.

Many years later, a spiritual healer told me that she had said it because of a plan, which my mother had devised in a past life, to prevent me from living freely and happily. The spiritual healer explained that I—or better, my soul—had done my mother wrong in a past life, many generations earlier, and my mother's soul had used this to have power over me because I still felt guilty about that mistake. She said that it was a power game that my mother's soul had played for several lifetimes.

This spiritual explanation gave me comfort by helping me see the sadness of this part of my story from a different perspective. When I was a child, my mother gave me the best support she was able to, given that she was struggling with an illness. So I granted myself permission to remember the good moments in our relationship: When I was eight, I made her a card that said, "For the Best Mami in the World." When she received it, her eyes were smiling, and I could see how happy she was.

The Final Curtain

The final act of my childhood was just a few days later. That day, my alarm woke me up at 5:30 a.m. It was an exceptionally warm morning in September in Munich. Still sleepy, I noticed a smell, bittersweet, unpleasant, and heavy. My mother had described this smell to me. It must have happened during the night. A lump started to grow in my throat. I got up and stepped carefully through the chaos of papers, books, and clothes on the floor, passing by my work table, which I had painted with colorful animals and palms years earlier. I opened the door to the hallway, not knowing what I'd find. The door to my mother's bedroom, where she slept with my stepfather, was closed. I took a deep breath and my shoulders relaxed a bit. I knew the doors to the two other rooms were locked so that the dog could not enter. I crossed the hallway and glanced at the stone staircase. It led to a loft with a huge storeroom, where innumerable files, documenting the legal proceedings between my mother and my father during the past sixteen years, were stored. In the loft was also a red wardrobe containing my mother's colorful dresses from the 1970s and her white wedding dress for the ceremony with my father, as well a little wooden replica of a shop, which my sister and I had played with. My parents had been divorced for seventeen years now.

I crept downstairs, careful not to make a sound. I was scared. In the hall, I passed photos of my mother, my sister, and me at a restaurant in France and also photos of us sitting on a beach. There were some old black-and-white pictures of my grandfather as a baby. And there were photos of my mother's second wedding; she was a beautiful young woman with long, dark hair and huge green eyes in a black dress with little flowers, and her two children, four and seven, stood in front of her.

As I entered the living room, I noticed that the blinds were down and that the key that normally was stuck in the lock of the front door was missing. Normally, we had a key in the door to keep Mimic, a strong and clever dog, from opening it. I glanced at the spot where we kept the other keys, and they had vanished from their usual place.

The telephone was not where it usually was, either. Wolfgang came toward me, his face swollen and his eyes red. The lump in my throat grew bigger.

"Go into the living room. I have to talk to you," he said. Like a robot, I followed him and sat down in one of the bulky armchairs that faced the TV. After some moments, he stepped in front of me. "Your mother died last night. You can see her if you want. I have kept her warm. Your sister will not be allowed to enter this house ever again." Anna had left the house to stay for a few days with Miriam, Wolfgang's younger daughter, to relieve the broiling conflict with Wolfgang. Our stepfather had imposed one demand after another on her and became each time more aggressive if she wanted to defend her needs. Anna had never intended to leave our home forever. "You can stay but only if you behave yourself." He was too close. My body wanted to move away. I blinked back my tears.

She has died, she has really died? You knew that I wanted to be with her in her last moments! Why didn't you wake me up? My anguished words were silent. *I won't be able to tell her good-bye? I will never be able to talk to her again, never ever see her again, never feel her embrace again?*

More tears sprang to my eyes. It took a greater effort to blink them back.

Don't cry, I told myself. *Just don't show anything.* I remained silent. I looked at Wolfgang. He stared back at me and said, "I will take the dog for a walk." Then he went outside with the dog, locking the entrance door behind him.

I just sat in the living room, surrounded by the weighty, dark sofa, the matching armchairs, the cupboard filled with antique books, and the delicate blue coffee service covered in images from the Bayeux tapestry. Suddenly, I realized that Anna did not yet know that Mami was dead. She would want to say good-bye to her. When my mother was on her deathbed, Anna lost her protection; Wolfgang could be as aggressive as he liked. I knew that it was important to her to see our mother's body. Wolfgang was away, so I looked for the phone. It was in the kitchen cupboard. With trembling fingers, I dialed Miriam's number.

"Hello?" Miriam answered in a sleepy voice. I felt the tears flow down my cheeks.

"Can I talk to Anna?" I said and my voice died away. I wasn't able to say more for the moment. Suddenly, I felt Wolfgang at my back. He pulled the phone out of my hand. I felt his aggression and his hate. I screamed. He did not say a word, just went away with the phone in his hands.

Alone in the living room again, I heard a key in the lock of the front door. A moment later, Anna rushed into the corridor. Miriam must have informed her about my phone call. Anna headed directly to the staircase to get to my mother's bedroom. Wolfgang came downstairs. "What has happened?" she said to him, tears running down her face.

The next moment, he was on top of her like an eagle that had caught its prey. He forced her to the ground and beat her, a big man fighting a much smaller young woman. He was Goliath and she was David—without a slingshot. The dull drumming of his fists on her body filled the corridor; her body sounded hollow. The dog was jumping around them and barking. I caught the look in Wolfgang's eyes. Their blue-white color showed hatred and revenge; they were cold and lifeless. Why did he hate us so much? I was certain that this time he would not stop beating my sister.

My feet had become part of the marble floor. I was a statue. My throat did not scream; I could barely breathe. I went outside my body. Was I in the cinema watching a horror movie? The hat stand fell to the ground on top of both of them. *This can't be real. This is my family. Please, dear God, do not allow this to be real.* Violence was normal in our house, but I had never expected a life-or-death struggle.

My sister's right hand grabbed something out of her pocket. *Pepper spray!* My mother had bought each of her daughters a canister to defend ourselves if we were attacked at night. The fine mist built up a cloud around both of them. For a moment, Wolfgang needed his hands to rub his eyes. Anna was able to get up. Together, we escaped to the driveway.

There we stood, not knowing what to do. Minutes later, two police officers arrived. One of them asked us, "What is going on here? Some neighbors called us." Anna explained to them that our mother had just died. She told them that she had been beaten up by our stepfather, who wouldn't allow her to live at home again. And she said that we didn't know where to go. They looked at us, two young women, not yet really adults, and entered the house. When they came back, they told us, "We cannot help in family affairs." They walked away and left us alone in the driveway.

I went with Anna to a doctor to take care of the injuries. Later, we went to the police station, where they told us again that they couldn't intervene in family affairs and that if Wolfgang wouldn't allow Anna to enter the house, she had no right to stay in her apparently former home.

Later that day, my mother's doctor visited in order to pronounce her dead. My sister accompanied her to say good-bye to my mother's corpse. I stood in the yard in front of the house; the lawn had a border of flowers, and leafy trees grew behind a neighbor's wall. Tears were running down my cheeks, but I could breathe freely again.

When the doctor left the house, she saw me standing there alone and crying. She came over and said, "Your mother was a wonderful woman. She endured unbearable suffering. Now she is free." I looked at her. The picture of my mother's suffering came to my mind; I saw her skeletonlike body with her eyes wide open, just like a rabbit in front of a cobra, when she could not breathe because of the metastases in her lungs. I had no idea what being free meant, but the energy of those words felt much better than remembering her terrified eyes and her pleading not to have to die when she was close to death. I saw myself lying in my bed, crying night after night and pleading for her life, begging God to let me die in her place. Now I had lost her forever, and yet there was the possibility that she finally had found something better.

At noon, my grandfather and his partner arrived. They passed by me, looking at me in silent reproach. My grandfather had always told Anna and me that we had to behave properly so that our mother wouldn't get cancer again. He seemed to see our mother's death as proof that we hadn't behaved properly. It never occurred to me to ask myself why he didn't see her death as proof that Wolfgang's infidelities had destroyed my mother. I did not know and did not even think to ask until years later. Now, I think that my grandfather needed somebody to blame to be able to bear the loss of his only child. I also think that it was easier to blame young women than a middle-aged man. At the time, I felt that I had done something wrong yet did not know what. Maybe it was my sheer existence.

My grandfather and his partner went for lunch with my stepfather. While Wolfgang was gone, I reentered the house and went into my room, together with my dog. I looked around and saw the chaos in the room, with clothes strewn on the floor. It was time to go. I packed a bag and called my only friend, Cornelia, who had finished school with me three months earlier and whom I met once in a while to take the dog for a walk. I asked her whether I could stay with her for a few days. I was afraid that she would say no. I felt unprotected and naked. It was the first time in my life that I had asked a friend for help. But she agreed and I left that afternoon. It did not enter my mind to stay with Anna because I hardly knew Miriam. As I exited my room, I saw that the door to my mother's bedroom was open. I glanced at the empty bed where my mother had lain for so many months, on which some rose leaves were spread; next to the bed was the oxygen cylinder, the bedpan, bottles of medications, foods, and injections. *Is this all that is left when someone dies?* I asked myself.

Ten minutes later, I arrived at my friend's house with my bag, feeling numb, missing my dog, whom I had left behind, and feeling guilty for leaving her. My heart was heavy. The movie of my life was over; this was the final scene. I never had been able to imagine what would happen after Mami's death. My family had been all that I had known. Would it become worse? I did not know what to expect or what to hope for.

My mother had gotten her wish. She had died three months after I had completed my school-leaving examination.

My decision to leave my mother's house and not to stay with Wolfgang was guided by my inner voice. I still can't explain how I had the strength to do this, because at this time I was a timid, highly introverted girl of nineteen who was usually too afraid to talk. I believe that I was protected by invisible energies, and I know that this step saved my life.

Five days later, Anna and I arrived at the cemetery. I had asked Michael, a new acquaintance I had met in a dance club a few months earlier, to accompany us. We needed an ally. There was a huge crowd of people whom I did not know. Desperately, I searched for a familiar face, for somebody who was friendly. I did not expect to see my father there. Even if he had wanted to show up, which was doubtful, neither Wolfgang nor my grandfather would have allowed him, due to their mutual hatred. Apparently, only colleagues of Wolfgang's were there. My grandfather and Wolfgang ignored us. It was the perfect setting to show the world that my sister and I were outcasts, the people to blame for my mother's illness and death. It did not seem fair. We were very young and had given all we could give. It had been hard to watch our mother die. In the front of the hall was my mother's coffin, a small, elegant thing. Michael, Anna, and I moved closer. The Protestant pastor started his homily. Suddenly, he said, "Most of the people involved did their best, but some members of the family failed." The words were meant for me and for my sister. Clearly, my stepfather had instructed the pastor to say the words! They hit me hard. My mother had said so often that her daughters were her reason for living. Her words seemed to have been forgotten.

My childhood was marked by conflict, rejection, abuse, and guilt. At nineteen, I did not know anything different. I was aware that sexual and physical violence were wrong. But I was unaware of the dynamics of abuse. I would go on to repeat the patterns I was familiar with because I wouldn't be able to recognize abuse. I couldn't imagine a better world. It took me many years to learn that other realities exist, that healthy relationships are possible, and that I have the power within myself to heal.

PART TWO
The Show Must Go On

Ignoring My Inner Voice

After my mother's death, I started a relationship with Michael, my acquaintance from the dance club. He had always been at the dance club when I visited it. I saw him there so often that we fell into a relationship. He was my first boyfriend. In the years that followed, I lived like a marionette, controlled by the strings pulled by my past, my father, my grandfather, and Michael. Deep feelings of guilt and shame for who I was and for disappointing my mother accompanied me. I wasn't able to distinguish who was good for me and what I needed.

My sister, Anna, cut contact with our grandfather and our stepfather and moved to Bonn with her boyfriend. We didn't get along well during the following years because each of us had to find her own way to deal with the traumatic experiences of our childhood.

Three years after my mother's death, my grandfather convinced me to get in touch with Wolfgang again. Feeling obliged to obey my grandfather, I agreed, and on a dark night in November 1996, I waited with Michael on a bridge in Munich. We were to meet Wolfgang and then have dinner in a Thai restaurant. The bridge was dark, lit by just a few streetlights, and empty except for parked cars. At the end of the bridge, the city continued, a ghostlike gray-beige silhouette of endless rows of houses. The air was filled with the slight smell of gasoline produced by the vehicles driven by endless commuters, a never-ending stream making its way home in the tunnel below after a hard day's work.

I saw a man and a dog approaching us. There they were!

What would happen now? I shifted from one leg to the other, my stomach cramping. It had been three years without contact—so many years without seeing my dog!

My grandfather had said, "Natalie, Wolfgang is like a father to you. You have known him nearly all your life. Forget the past. Your mother would want you to stay in touch with him."

I had never told my grandfather that Wolfgang had beaten Anna on the day of our mother's death. My sister had told him, and he had not believed her. I did not think that my words could change his mind. He lived in his own world and wanted to see Wolfgang as a good partner for my mother. He rejected any information that would have contradicted his vision of the world. I had learned that my opinion did not count and that I had to obey the adults—and so I did. My grandfather had labeled my sister as the difficult person, as the one who couldn't do anything right. This made his life comfortable. He didn't want to see the truth.

Despite his failings, I did not want to disappoint my grandfather. He already had suffered so much because my mother—his daughter—had died.

One part of my heart was excited now. I would see my dog again! The other part was fearful. I did not want to see my stepfather.

Suddenly, Mimic, my dog, started to wag her tail and howl. She threw her head back and made a sound full of longing and joy that came from deep within her body. Arriving in front of me, she jumped up, put her forepaws on my shoulders, and gave me a kiss. It was as though nothing had changed. Then I turned around and saw Wolfgang. He looked the same, with his gray hair and blue-gray eyes. He said hello and kissed me on my mouth as usual. As always, it was displeasing, and I wanted to run away. But I told myself, *He is like a father. It is normal that your father does this.* Then I introduced Michael and Wolfgang. I was glad that I was not alone. Michael was my protection. With him by my side, Wolfgang could not explode.

We went to the Thai restaurant at the other end of the street for dinner. It was a well-known place with large windows overlooking the street and large golden Buddha statues decorated with lotus flowers. My family had celebrated many birthdays there.

I felt happy that my dog was under the table. I had missed her so much. I looked at Wolfgang's face across the table and felt a strange sensation; I'd known him for a long time yet I longed to run away. Then I heard my mother's voice in my head: *He is like a father to you. You have to accept him as he is.* I had known Wolfgang since I was a year old. I told myself that it was good to have contact with my stepfather and that my mother would appreciate it.

"The death of your mother was horrible for me," he began after ordering the drinks and the meal. "I miss her a lot. I carry her wedding ring with me."

He put his bunch of keys on the table and showed us the small silver ring of my mother. I thought that he must have really felt something for her. At the same moment, a picture of someone else, a blonde woman, popped up in my mind. Wolfgang had chosen her to care for my mother in the weeks prior to her death. In her late twenties, with long blonde hair and huge breasts, she was just the type of woman with whom he had affairs while my mother was alive. On her deathbed, she saw her husband interacting with the type of woman he seemed to favor. How had my mother felt in those moments? A shudder ran down my spine.

Wolfgang's voice interrupted my thoughts: "You know, I had profound conversations with your mother in the weeks before her death. She shared with me thoughts about life that were so deeply poetic. It was great to have that experience."

I thought about my conversations with my mother during her last weeks. Rarely able to speak, she fought with her own fear of dying while under the influence of strong painkillers. Countless nights in the darkness of my bedroom, I begged God to allow me to die instead of her, because she was so desperate to continue living. Only in the shelter of the night did I allow myself to cry, and the tears rolled down my face as though they would never stop. My heart was breaking because of the suffering of my mother. Yet she continued dying and I felt worthless because I could not alleviate her pain.

While Wolfgang talked about her last days, I suddenly saw an image in my imagination: my mother next to Wolfgang, he embracing her, she talking about life and death calmly. It was such a comforting image. I felt relieved because it seemed that my mother had finally found peace in her relationship with him. It gave me hope that she had died happily. I wanted to believe this and my tension softened.

"What are you doing these days?" Wolfgang asked, looking at me.

"I am studying industrial engineering. You know, I started with mechanical engineering, but I did not like it much and so I switched majors." It was a half-truth. The first year after the death of my mother, I had attended class only occasionally. I had experienced sleeping problems and severe nightmares. As a result, I had missed many classes.

During my third term, other students had been able to draw mechanical machines and solve highly sophisticated calculations, while I had not been able to follow the professor's words and had felt overwhelmed. I had tried desperately to catch up, and it had been only luck that I had passed my exams. At the end of the fourth term, I had decided that the risk that I would flunk was too great. So I had changed my course of study.

"I see my father every two weeks and help him with his business." My father had been a manager in the human resources department of a corporation until he became a consultant to businesses as a leadership trainer. "He has not changed at all. He still tells his bad stories about Mami every time I see him." I suddenly felt very sad.

"Well, that's what he always did. Just don't listen to him," Wolfgang replied curtly.

I nodded. I knew this sentence so well. I had heard it all throughout my childhood.

I stayed in touch with Wolfgang. My stepfather wanted me to think that his relationship with my mother had had a good end, with my mother finding peace. And I wanted to believe him, even though I knew that Wolfgang had betrayed my mother several times. Despite the fact that he had bought flowers for each wedding anniversary, I believe that he had been not a loving husband to my mother but a secure harbor for her. After she lost her beauty, she lost any hope she might have had of finding a better man.

A few weeks later, Wolfgang invited Michael and me to his house. Wolfgang still lived in the same house he had lived in with my mother. I was returning home for the first time in three years. What would it be like? I had no idea.

When we arrived, Wolfgang opened the door while Mimic jumped and barked, happily wagging her tail. Once again, I stood in the hallway. All over the walls were photos showing my mother on every occasion—as a young woman in the 1970s, in a bikini enjoying a glass of wine in front of a van, and in dozens of other poses. It was a shrine to the memory of my mother. I was overwhelmed and shocked. I could not see any white spot on the wall, only photos. Step by step, I moved forward cautiously. Then I saw two photos in the middle of the corridor wall, visible to each and every visitor: my mother's corpse in her short nightdress, which exposed her emaciated legs. At that point, I had never heard of the custom of taking a photo of the dead body of a family member. For me, it was another example of Wolfgang's strange relationship with the camera. Shocked, I glanced at Michael. It felt so weird. He had not yet noticed it. *Well, at least he didn't hang up the photo of Mami without a cheek!* I tried to calm down. *What is waiting for me behind the other doors of my old home?* I asked myself silently. I didn't really want to find out.

"There are a lot of photos of Mami," I said to Wolfgang.

"Yes, I want her close to me."

We moved on into the salon, where the round marble table was set with the dishes decorated with wild roses in dusky pink that my mother had loved so much. In the middle of the table stood a huge plate with some delicious-looking cakes, the kind we had always had on Sundays with my grandfather and his partner when my mother was alive. The table looked inviting, yet it was strange to be in my mother's house knowing that she would never return to it. We sat down and Wolfgang asked us what we wanted. While distributing the cakes, Wolfgang said, "Later, we can watch some videos from our last trip to France with your mother."

I glanced at Michael. He did not seem to object. "Sure," I said.

After finishing the cakes, Wolfgang turned the heavy chairs around to face the TV and inserted the first tape. My mother appeared onscreen, sitting in a camping chair at a table full of French delicacies. She said something. At the sound of my mother's voice, Mimic started to run around the room nervously. She whined. She'd never find her.

Later, Michael and I drove home.

"Did you see the photo of my mother's corpse?"

"No. But the number of photos is really strange. He seems to be an odd man," he replied, concentrating on the traffic.

"I need you with me when I meet him. I don't want to be alone with him, and the house is spooky to me. Do you mind?"

"No, that's not a problem."

Our contact continued for the following three years. As a child, I had regarded him as being as important as a father, and I had lived under the same roof with him for sixteen years. He hadn't changed at all, yet I was not yet prepared to face reality and see his true character. I still acted like a loyal child, wanting to fulfill the wishes of my late mother and my grandfather.

Then I finished my studies, and Wolfgang said to me, "I want to give you a special present for finishing your studies." I looked at him with inner tension and he continued, "Your sister traveled to London with your mother after her school-leaving examination. You never had that opportunity because your mother died right after you finished school. That's why I now want to take you to Thailand." I imagined myself in Thailand with him, alone without my boyfriend. I wanted to scream no! and run, but my head said, *You cannot reject a present. He is like a father. What if he really just wants to do something nice for you?* I said yes. Silently, I hoped that he'd forget about his plan.

Some weeks later, Wolfgang phoned me to say that he wanted to go shopping with me for Christmas. I met him on a cold day two weeks before Christmas at the Marienplatz in Munich. Suddenly, he grabbed my arm and pushed me inside the travel agency with the comment, "Let's book our trip now."

A moment later, I sat in a travel agency, Wolfgang at my side. The travel agent, a friendly-looking woman with brown hair and a smile, sat opposite us behind a huge white desk. The walls were light green and the room had panoramic windows, through which throngs of people could be seen rushing about to complete their Christmas shopping. Behind the travel agent, the shelf was filled with catalogues of endless white beaches with green palms or giant mountains covered with green jungle. I halfheartedly listened to Wolfgang's explanation about traveling to Thailand with me.

Wolfgang and the travel agent went through the catalogues, and the travel agent asked in her warm voice, "Do you want a double room or two single rooms?"

Wolfgang replied, "A double room."

I spoke up: "No, I want a single room."

He was slightly angry and said that this would cost more. Although I insisted, I thought for a moment about what the lady might think of me, a daughter who did not want to sleep in the same room as her father. I felt guilty yet I ignored it. It was the first time in my life that I had said no to him.

He replied, "Well, if you want a single room, then you have to travel with me for three weeks instead of two."

What kind of logic is that? I was too horrified to speak the words aloud or contradict him. I told myself that I would survive this trip, that it was only a trip, and I asked myself why I saw everything as so dark. He was just doing what a father does.

That day, I was listening to my inner voice, but I wasn't able to follow it. Five weeks later, I was on an airplane to Bangkok.

The monotonous noise of the engines filled my ears; outside the small windows was complete darkness. The darkness inside the plane was broken by dots of light above seats where people were reading and the dimmed light above each window. Most people sat in more-or-less comfortable positions in their seats, trying to catch a bit of sleep after having finished an airplane dinner. Wolfgang and I had started our travel in Munich. From there, we had flown to Zurich, and within one hour we had changed to a plane to Bangkok, which took off shortly before midnight. I had an aisle seat and he sat next to me.

I was excited about going to Thailand; I had always wanted to visit it. But something felt wrong. The voice in my head tried to calm me down: *Why are you so suspicious? He is like a father. It is all right to go to Asia. Mami would have loved you to do that. She always wanted you to be close to him.*

Wolfgang's voice interrupted my inner dialogue: "If you want, you can put your head on my shoulder." His eyes had a strange, unfamiliar look, and he tapped his shoulder.

Inside, I screamed, *No, never!* My body became rigid and I replied coldly, "No, thank you, I could not sleep like that." I wanted to move as far away from him as I could, and I managed to sit down on the floor and put my head on the seat. But I still could not sleep, and after what felt like an eternity, I got up. On my way to the bathroom, I peeked through the window of the emergency exit. Far below my feet, in the midst of complete darkness, there was a beautiful star—a magical city full of light. *That must be New Delhi.* I stood at the window, inhaled the beauty and the peace of the view, and imagined for a moment the miracles that might be happening right now in this faraway city. I would have loved to have stayed in that darkness forever. Later, I returned to the darkness at my seat, and the plane landed some hours later in Bangkok.

The next day, I stood at the window of my Bangkok hotel room. It was early morning, and only a thin pane of glass separated me from the Chao Phraya River, which wound its way through the city below. The gray-blue of the river and the green of the palm trees rose up from the mist, and in the distance I could see the red rooftops of temples beyond the dreamlike shadows of skyscrapers.

Am I really here? The hotel room was elegant, with a weighty desk of red lacquered wood on one side, a bed with white blankets on the other side, and a beige carpet. I had never had such an elegant hotel room before. I wore an ankle-length, wraparound salmon-colored skirt of a delicate lace material with flower embroidery. I had bought the skirt especially for my first holiday in Asia because I had read that it was important to wear long skirts to respect the Thai culture. I felt feminine. I was thrilled about the prospect of visiting the temples and getting in touch with the culture. I had never been in Asia before. So far, I had visited only places in Europe and the United States. Thailand was something new. Even though I did not feel good about the fact that I was visiting the country with Wolfgang, I was excited about seeing Thailand.

I looked at the pocket watch that Michael had given me: 7:30 a.m., time for breakfast. I took the elevator to meet Wolfgang in the lobby. When we had arrived at the hotel the evening before, I had not even asked him his room number and had cautiously avoided showing him my own room number.

From the lobby, Wolfgang walked with me outside to the terrace for breakfast. I was still excited about being in Thailand.

But something was wrong. What was it? We sat at a table for two facing the water, and then I went to the buffet. There were exotic fruits laid out that I had never seen before. Fascinated, I chose fresh papaya and returned to my seat. Wolfgang followed and I forced myself to talk to him.

"How did you sleep?"

Frowning, he said, "Horribly. That air-conditioning is terrible. I know that I will get ill. I could not turn it off." He pressed his lips together. I gazed at the streaming water of the river and tasted the papaya. Instantly, I fell in love with its sweet taste. *How often have I heard this complaint from him!*

"It's a wonderful view from the terrace, isn't it?"

"Yes, it's nice. Well, I am not at all eager to meet the people from our tour group. They're going to be a bunch of bores." I knew that he did not like people. Did he have any friends? He and my mother had lived like hermits. When we had lived with him, my sister and I rarely had visitors because he did not like them.

Ten minutes later, we waited in front of the hotel for our tour group. I saw a group of twelve people in the distance. Two women were in their late thirties, and the rest of the group were in their sixties and seventies. I was by far the youngest member. The tour guide introduced herself. She was an energetic woman in her early thirties with wild and curly dark hair; she appeared to be Arab. We entered the river taxi and crossed the river. In the distance, the impressive white silhouette of the temple Wat Arun became visible against the light blue sky. When the boat arrived at the landing bridge, we disembarked.

Wolfgang was the last to leave the ship and hung back a few feet from the rest of the group. We walked up some stairs, and two men who wore two boa constrictors wrapped around their shoulders approached us to ask for money. Shocked by seeing snakes so close, I pressed myself to the wall of the pier to avoid them. We entered the temple and walked around. The peace and calm of the place entered me, and I enjoyed the yellow and green ornaments that decorated its stupa, or dome. Wolfgang was always slow and always behind me. I felt observed; when I turned around, I caught him giving me a strange look. He had his camera in his hand, yet I had the impression that he was not interested in the temple. I tried to stay away from him and listened with rapt attention to the guide and her stories.

That night, I called Michael and told him that I did not feel good about the situation with Wolfgang. He was not interested in talking to me because he had assumed that he had his freedom while I was away. Later, I stood a long time at the window of my room and looked at the nearby bridge. I still could feel the eyes of Wolfgang on my back. I felt dirty, so horribly dirty. For a moment, I thought about what it must feel like to jump from the bridge just to end the dirtiness, to jump and not feel the hurt anymore.

I told myself that I was crazy: he was just like a father and I was being ungrateful to him. I was in Asia, on the journey of my dreams. I did not want to live in a nightmare.

The next morning, we visited the Grand Palace in Bangkok. We arrived there by water taxi, and when we reached the pier, we left the boat and stood on a little wooden terrace, which was like a fragile cage above the water. Metal plates served as a roof. The huge holes in the rotten planks gave us a view of the river and its dirty gray water, in which floated plastic bottles and rubbish and sometimes a snake or a dead animal. I was not able to see a shore or a direct entry to the river, only endless wooden terraces. It seemed like the river was a dead end; if you fell in, you would surely drown. A little cat was playing on the terrace. I sent a wish out into the Universe that it would never fall into the river. On the terrace, we passed by woks placed on stones; below the woks, wood fires burned. The women sitting at the woks looked at us with curiosity. Apparently, we were standing in the outdoor kitchens of the families who lived on these wooden constructions above the river.

After walking for a while, we reached the street, and I was deafened by the noise of the tuk-tuks, or motorcycle taxis, which took tourists from one place to another. We entered the temple; suddenly, there was nothing but silence. The complex was huge, with red roofs covered with gold. Some giant bonsais completed the picture. I walked off and started to explore the temple alone when I got a strange feeling that I was being spied on. When I turned around, I saw Wolfgang in the middle of the group while the guide was explaining something. Yet he was not listening, nor was he filming the temple. His camera was pointing at me; he was filming me. I gave him an angry look and gestured for him to stop. He knew that I did not like to be filmed, but he had an obsession. I turned around and moved away as far as I could get.

Later, I turned around again and caught him pointing his camera at me. I started to hide behind Buddha statues and bonsai trees to have a bit of privacy. My mother seemed to say softly, as she had innumerable times in my childhood, *Natalie, you have to take him as he is. You have to adapt; you cannot change him.* As a child, I had asked myself why I always had to do the adapting, yet in the end I knew that she was right: he would never change.

Three days later, we had just arrived at a new hotel. It was nighttime and I stood in the tiny hotel corridor, which was illuminated by dim light. I took a deep breath and knocked reluctantly at the door in front of me. Wolfgang had given me his room number and asked me to meet him there before dinner. He opened the door. Hot and humid air hit my face. He must have turned off the air-conditioning. A moldy smell entered my nostrils. I wanted to turn my head with disgust. How relieved I was that I did not share a room with him. I silently asked myself how he could tolerate the smell of sweat or the dead air or the heat. The temperature was still over 100 degrees Fahrenheit outside. I looked at his face. Although rivers of sweat ran down his face, he had a towel around his neck; he often did this to protect his throat.

"I can't go to dinner," he said reproachfully. "I am ill. It's because of the air-conditioning." The air-conditioning again. I looked at him. Was he really ill? Or just hot? During the day, he seemed to have felt well.

"I'm sorry to hear that. I hope you'll feel better after a rest," I said politely. He closed the door and I walked down the corridor. It would be the first time that I'd be with the other members of the travel group without Wolfgang. A strange mixture of emotions bubbled up: I was relieved that he would not be at dinner, I felt bad that I somehow felt so angry about his filming me all the time, and I felt awkward because I was not used to talking to people I did not know.

The dinner was in the Chinese restaurant of the hotel. Entering the restaurant, I saw that the tables for the travel group were in the rear of the room, near the windows, which were covered by thick pale green curtains. All the other tables were empty; only our group was there. Two huge, round tables were reserved for us.

I took a seat at the table on the right and sat down next to an elderly lady, Caroline. I felt comfortable with Caroline even though I had never said anything more than good morning to her. An elegant woman in her late sixties, she was also from Munich. Her long dark gray hair had silver streaks in it. Her warm, friendly eyes gave me confidence. She was traveling with a friend, a German woman who was now living in the United States. Her friend had short blonde hair and wore mostly practical T-shirts and pants. When I sat down at Caroline's side, she smiled and asked me whether I was alone that evening. "Yes," I replied, "Wolfgang is ill." The food was served and various vegetarian dishes piled up around my plate. I asked myself whether I would ever be able to eat all the food; I was embarrassed to receive so much attention. I would have preferred to have been invisible. Caroline was conversing with her friend, and I listened to them.

Unable to eat all the plates of food, I offered my vegetarian dishes to the other people. Suddenly, Caroline turned and put a hand on my arm. She looked into my eyes and said in a very low voice so that nobody else could hear, "I am sorry. I do not want to invade your privacy. Yet there is a question my friend and I are wondering about all the time. Is it OK if I ask you a personal question?"

I looked at her, puzzled. *What are they wondering about me?*

"Sure, you can ask me," I replied.

"My friend and I have been observing you and Wolfgang for the past few days. It's impossible not to see that he is always looking at you amorously. But you appear to be very young. So we are wondering whether you are a couple."

My heart sank low. My soul wanted to scream. So she had perceived it, too! She was telling me the truth that I had not wanted to believe. My body went stiff. I felt like running away. But where could I go? I was in a foreign country. I did not know the language. I took a breath, looked at her, and tried to defend the last bit of dignity I had. "No, he is my stepfather," I said. "He has known me since I was just a year old. He is a father to me. My mother died several years ago. This trip is his gift for finishing my studies."

She looked at me and replied gently, "Fine." Then she turned to her friend and picked up the thread of their conversation.

I sat at her side, fighting back tears. I felt that I had not defended my dignity. Wolfgang wanted to put me in my mother's place. How could he do this to me? He was like a father. How could he do this to my mother? I was her daughter. What would people think about me? My head was filled with a thunderstorm of questions. Humiliation and anger flooded my body. I felt so dirty, so deeply ashamed. I saw a big sign on my forehead—Incest Victim—for the whole world to see. I longed to be invisible. What had I done wrong? What had I done to provoke this? Why was he doing this to me?

I got up from the table with a smile on my face. I was well practiced at not showing anything. Inside, I was stuck in a swamp. I would try desperately to get out, but the more I fought, the deeper I sank. Already my legs and arms could not move, trapped as they were in a grave of mud that came up to my throat. It would not be much longer until the mud covered my mouth, cutting off my breath. Like a robot, I went to the reception desk and asked for the connection number to make calls to Germany. I had to phone my boyfriend. I needed a lifeline.

I called his number, the phone rang, and he answered. "Michael, do you know what just happened?" I asked him, tears running down my face. "I went to dinner and a lady from the group asked me whether Wolfgang and I were a couple. I feel horrible."

He replied that he was sick and tired of my calls. He did not want me to phone him every day. I should leave him alone. I listened to him, not knowing what to say. My phone calls to him were my only source of oxygen. I needed them desperately. At that stage of my life, Michael was the person closest to me. My sister had moved away and we didn't get along very well.

I answered, "But just right now I need to hear your voice."

His reply was short and direct: "Well, now you have heard it." He hung up.

I looked outside the window and saw the beauty of the paradise I was visiting: fascinating, colorful temples with red roofs, exquisite Buddha statues, thousands of years of stories that transmitted peace and stillness, and colorful markets offering tasty, exotic foods. I might as well have been in purgatory.

I returned to my room and lay down on my bed, tears running down my cheeks, feeling completely empty, asking myself whether it would be better to end my life then and there. *What would my mother have thought of me? What have I done wrong? Is it really worthwhile to continue living?*

The next morning, I got up and went to breakfast, weighed down by the knowledge that Wolfgang felt something for me that he shouldn't. This was the truth. I could not embellish the situation. My intuition had been right! When I entered the hotel restaurant, I saw him sitting at a table eating a plate full of scrambled eggs and bacon; he seemed to eat with gusto. I wanted to shout at him that he should leave me alone. I wanted to grab his shoulders and shake him. I felt betrayed. How could I deal with this situation?

I was a bird in a golden cage, a helpless marionette in the hands of a puppeteer who did not care about anything. If I told him I was angry, I'd be called ungrateful. *He who pays the piper calls the tune*: this was what my mother, my father, and my grandfather had taught me. I had not known the price of this trip. I'd thought that he was a father to me and would act like a father. How could I escape? I did not see any way out. I looked at the people in my tour group. What would happen if they found out? A shudder ran down my spine. What if they already sensed it? I felt guilty. What had I done to turn Wolfgang into a lecher? Suddenly, the wonderful skirt that I had bought for the trip felt dirty.

In that moment, I built an invisible wall around me, a psychic fortress to protect myself. I told myself, *Just don't feel anything.* My face showed only a slight smile. The mask that I had used all my life was my powerful protection. *Just pretend that everything is normal; at least, the facade is clean.*

Suddenly, the phrase, "He is like a father to you," which I had heard many times from my mother and my grandfather, lost its meaning. *No, he is not like a father to me.* I told my mother silently that a father does not behave this way. Wolfgang was a selfish old man who wanted to abuse me. My shoulders felt stiff. I would not give him any chance to touch me. From now on, I would stop being nice to him and would defend myself. I would stop seeing him as a sad, lonely man. He had known perfectly well what he had wanted from me when he offered me this trip. I felt anger flare up inside me. It helped me set my limits. I would talk to the other members of my tour group. I would talk to Wolfgang. But if he touched me, I'd kill myself. This was my weapon to save my dignity. What would have happened if I had stayed in a double room with him? I tried not to think about it, just congratulated myself for insisting on a single room. With tense shoulders, I sat down at the table.

"I feel horrible. I still have a fever," Wolfgang said reproachfully.

I looked into his eyes and felt disgust. Should I believe him? I knew that I looked different when I had a fever. "You will get better," I said coldly and got up to get fresh pineapple and papaya. Tasting the fruit gave me some comfort, so I concentrated on that. I avoided looking at Wolfgang. We went to the bus together, and I sat down in our usual row, next to him. The closeness of his body was unbearable.

That day, we went to a national park for a hike. When the bus stopped, I got off before Wolfgang. As usual, he was the last to leave the bus. I did not care anymore about whether I would hurt him or whether I was ungrateful. I just thought about what would be best for me in the situation. I walked with Christine, an agile woman in her late seventies with short blonde hair and sunburned skin; her energy was that of a woman in her forties. She traveled alone and she told me that she had always traveled alone, even when her husband was still alive. I had never heard of a married person traveling alone, and I admired her independence. But I also wondered whether Christine and her husband had really loved each other. Walking by her side was a relief; I started to enjoy the scenery of the park, with its impressive rocks and the exotic deep green trees. Wolfgang's fever did not stop him from going on a hike, and after breakfast he never again mentioned his fever.

For the next few days, I repeated this ritual. I took advantage of Wolfgang's snail-like pace to jump off the bus first, and I walked with either Christine or Caroline. Wolfgang would look at me longingly, like a dog who begged for food but knew that it might not get anything.

Three days later, we arrived in Chiang Mai, and the group separated. When I said good-bye to Caroline, she gave me her business card and said, "I'd love to get together with you in Munich." I felt thankful that this warmhearted and kind woman wanted to stay in touch with me, even though I could not understand why she wanted to be my friend.

I nodded and said, "Yes, I'll contact you."

She flew back to Munich, and Wolfgang and I flew south. I had hardly spoken a word to him in the past few days; the atmosphere between us was cold. I noticed that my tone was icy when I spoke to him. For the first time in my life, I did not care that I was rude; I did not feel guilty about my behavior. I had to do it to defend my dignity. Had I known his hidden desires before the trip, I would never have agreed to travel with him. When we left Nakhon Si Thammarat Airport, I saw the bus that stood in front of the terminal waiting for us. I looked at it and saw the possibility to sever the last connection to Wolfgang. He had always insisted on switching the air-conditioning off for our seats. This was my chance to escape. I turned to him and said, "I'll sit in a single row now. I can't be without air-conditioning. It is just too hot for me." Then I rushed onto the bus without waiting for his reply. I would not give him an opportunity to argue. I chose a seat in the very back. From the window, I could observe how Wolfgang crawled like a slug from the airport to the bus. He entered and sat down in a seat in the front. I turned the air-conditioning on. Even though a part of me pitied him because he seemed so lonely, I was relieved.

When we arrived at the hotel, our tour guide told us that we would have a free afternoon. I followed behind her and was the first one to get the keys. On the way to my room, I told Wolfgang that I was horribly tired because of the early flight and that I would just go to my room to sleep. He looked at me and I could feel his suppressed anger. He had had other expectations. Slowly, I started to enjoy our little game. Before this trip, I would never have believed that I could be so cruel—but being cruel felt much better than being a victim. That day, I enjoyed an afternoon in the anonymity of my room without having him staring at me. I was able to breathe again.

Two days later, we arrived back at Munich Airport in the early morning. When our suitcases arrived, Wolfgang and I walked to the exit together without a word. In the arrivals hall, Michael was waiting for me. What a relief! I looked at Wolfgang and gave him the obligatory kiss on the mouth. Then I rushed to Michael's side. The nightmare was over.

While Michael and I drove away, I said, "It was so horrible! I don't know what to do now. I don't want to lose contact with Mimic!"

Michael replied without much interest, "Wait and see. Nothing bad will come of this. But you do have really strange fathers."

I sighed. He was right. Something felt wrong about my fathers, yet I could not put my finger on exactly what it was—despite the fact that I had spent my vacation avoiding my step-father's advances. I was still confused. Other people talked differently about their fathers. Was my father—either one—a good father? What was a good father? What rights did a father have? What were the limits? Was I allowed to say no to my father? I was starting to ask the right questions.

The trip to Thailand had two different aspects to it. It opened my eyes to the true nature of Wolfgang's intentions and to his manipulations. I finally understood that he was unscrupulous, unethical, and valued only possessions and money. He didn't care about others; he cared only about himself. After the trip, I withdrew from this relationship and didn't contact him for several months.

On the same trip, I got in touch with the Asian culture and Buddhism. It was my first step in defining my spiritual truth. In my family, spirituality was forbidden and ridiculed. In Thailand, I connected with spirituality for the first time in my life, and I became curious about it, even though it would take many years until I started to practice it.

Yearning for Love

After my mother's death, I established regular contact with my father. My sister, following arguments between her and our father, cut contact with him shortly after my mother's death. When Anna moved away from Munich, she did not give him her new address. As usual, my father blamed my mother.

I did not yet have a clear opinion about my father and I longed for his love, so I visited him and his wife every second Saturday and worked for my father's business. My father was not skilled with computers, so I was the one to prepare the presentation material for his leadership trainings. I did this work for the next seven years. The visits were mostly a repetition of a scenario that unfolded in December 1998, when I was invited to have Christmas lunch at my father and Gabriela's place. Michael was not invited because my father did not like him.

I left Michael's apartment and crossed the street to go to my car. Gray-white snow covered the pavement and the branches of the few trees that grew in the gardens of the apartment buildings. The street was nearly empty—no traffic and no drivers desperately looking for a parking spot. During Christmas, the nonlocal residents who worked at the big companies in Munich visited their families and left the streets abandoned. Munich was a booming economic center and attracted professionals from all over Germany and abroad. I scraped the snow from my car window, started the engine, and put the music on. As usual, I passed by the channel of the Nymphenburg Palace, which was framed by majestic trees; at this time of year, the tree branches were bare. A couple of people were curling—a sport that involves sliding stones across ice—on the frozen channel, huge scarves covering their faces. A vendor's booth offered hot spiced wine and roasted chestnuts. A few small children took their first tentative steps on the new ice skates they had gotten as gifts on Christmas Eve. I made a turn at the Nymphenburg Palace and glanced at the beauty of its baroque facade.

When I was nearly there, I sighed and turned the music up a bit. What awaited me this time at my father's place? Five minutes later, I arrived at a friendly-looking two-floor apartment house. It was painted a light beige and had huge balconies in the front, facing the garden. I parked the car, went to the door, and rang the bell.

"*Hel-*lo," responded my father slowly.

"It's me," I replied. I took a breath. I could not stand his voice. It seemed to invade me. I had felt this for a long time, but it was only recently that I was able to put my feeling into words. *Why am I so overly sensitive?* I went upstairs, where he waited for me at the open door. He was still tall but now he was corpulent, and his dark hair had gray strands in it. He still wore glasses and his eyes, as always, were filled with suffering.

"Merry Christmas, Papa!" I said. He embraced me and gave me a kiss, scratching my cheek with his moustache and holding on to me too long.

I went into the kitchen, where Gabriela was cooking, said hello, and took my usual place in the kitchen at the window. She was just dropping a handful of penne in the boiling water. "*Uno, due, tre* . . . ," she counted in Italian. "It will take only a few more minutes. Just have a seat at the table," she said and gestured for me to go into the other room. The dining room was really a small passageway between the kitchen and the living room that was occupied by an ebony octagonal table and a seat bench. I sat down at my place near the window while my father lit two white candles in heavy silver candleholders.

He looked at them and said, "I am so lucky to have found

these wonderful silver candleholders. It is not easy to find such elegant work. What do you think?"

I just nodded; he talked about the candleholders every time I visited him.

Looking at his watch, he said, "You see, this is a special watch. The clockwork was made in Switzerland. It cost 3,000 deutsche marks. I am so glad that I could afford to buy it." I looked at his watch without interest. He knew that I did not wear watches.

Why does he care so much about money? I asked silently. I guess it's because his own father never made much money as a tailor. And of course Papa's family had even less money during World War II.

My father continued, "You have to understand about watches. In the business world, it is highly important that you know about watches. People will judge you based on the watch you wear. My watch helps business."

Well, then my career will be a failure, I told myself silently. Aloud, I said, "I don't like watches."

He got up and went into the living room. Then he came back with a gift-wrapped package and said, "Here, this is your Christmas present. Open it." He handed me the package. It was hefty and I opened it cautiously. It was a book. I turned it around. On the cover were pictures of watches. *All About Swiss Watches* was the title. I did not know what to think. One part of me was angry. Why would he give me something that he knew I would not like? But it was a present, and my father had already mentioned on other occasions that I should not look a gift horse in the mouth. I felt powerless. Yet another unwelcome gift from my father. Nice girl that I was, I thanked him and forced a smile.

He replied with a triumphant look, "You will need it."

Gabriela was serving the food, *penne all'arrabbiata* and green salad. What a relief—for a while, I would not be alone with him.

After lunch, Gabriela as usual retreated into the bedroom without a word. My father wanted to talk to me, and as always she was not allowed to be involved in these conversations. I entered the living room, which was suffused with sunlight. My father already sat on the white sofa, angled in front of the window. I sat down at the other end of the sofa.

"Gabriela wanted to celebrate Christmas with her elderly father in Como. If you were me, where would you spend Christmas?"

"I'd spend Christmas one year in Munich and the other year with my partner's family," I replied. I knew that he would not like my honest answer, and that gave me some satisfaction. I wished that he would celebrate Christmas in Italy. That way, I could spend my Christmas without him. The prospect made me smile.

He gave me an angry look and said firmly, "Well, for me, the only right answer is that we all spend Christmas together in Munich." His voice was full of self-congratulation. He continued speaking; as always, I tried not to listen. I focused my attention on the beautiful birch tree that grew outside the balcony and the crystal clear winter sky. Suddenly, he moved closer to me.

He's done it again—invaded my space.

In the next moment, he was at my side. "As my daughter, it is your obligation to celebrate Christmas with me," he said and gave me an aggressive push, his right hand against my upper arm.

Why does he always have to touch me? Why can't he respect my personal space?

Then he started in on my mother. For my father, forgiveness didn't exist. *Why does he return again and again to incidents that happened more than twenty years ago?* I pulled away from him.

"Your mother's final insult to me was allowing you to go to college. Higher education is neither necessary nor desirable for a woman. An apprenticeship in a bank would have been sufficient." I was silent. I had always been good at school, and I liked my field, industrial engineering. It had always been clear to my mother and me that I would pursue higher education. I had never questioned it. Why shouldn't I study? I shrank farther away from him. The end of the sofa came closer. I gazed out the window.

When will he finish with his lecture? When will he stop bad-mouthing my mother? Slowly, the darkness was overtaking the sky. He said, "Your mother always worked to alienate my daughters from me." I was getting angry. I had told him often that my mother had done nothing to alienate us from him.

When will he believe me? She had been dead more than six years. I visited him every other weekend. What more could he ask for? Contrary to what my father asserted, my mother had always pushed me to stay in touch with him: "He is your father. It is better for you to see him. You have to adapt and take him as he is." My mother's words rang in my head. My outrage began to build. I would not allow my father to speak poorly of my mother.

"My mother never tried to alienate us from you!" Should I tell him the truth? I recalled that when I was five, I had locked myself in the bathroom; I didn't want to see my father. Mami had to be her most persuasive to get me to come out. It wasn't about my mother. It was about him and the way he treated my sister and me.

I was now a twenty-six-year-old woman, and for my late mother's sake, I wanted to speak the truth. But I knew that it wouldn't matter what I said; he would never believe me. Nothing had changed. No matter what I did, it was wrong. And as always, he ignored my comment.

"Well, anyway, she died of cancer. That was God's punishment for leaving me." As always, my father interpreted any doctrine so that it served him. My mother was the sinner because she had left him. He ignored the fact that he had remarried after a divorce, which was not acceptable to the Catholic Church either.

Papa got up from the sofa to inform Gabriela that she was allowed to enter the living room. Our conversation was finished. I sat alone on the sofa for a moment. My maternal grandfather always said that I should just let him talk. His words should go in one ear and out the other. I did my best, but my father's words about my mother hurt as much as if he had rammed a knife in my heart.

I reflected on the fact that I had visited my father for years and did not often challenge him because I yearned for his love. I had hoped that he would change after the death of my mother, that he would let go of his hatred. I had also wanted to fulfill my mother's wish that I stay in touch with him. But over the years, contact with my father had grown more and more unbearable as I slowly became aware of how his negative energy affected me. I was not yet ready to give up on him, but occasionally I rebelled against him.

When I left my father's home later that evening, I was still angry.

When I traveled to Thailand with Wolfgang, I missed my father's sixtieth birthday. My trip to Thailand was a secret, because my father didn't know that I was in touch with Wolfgang, but I knew that he viewed my absence on his birthday as an affront.

When I returned from Thailand, I visited him as usual on a Saturday. I sat again at the ebony table with my father and Gabriela. The two candles in the elegant silver candleholders lent a delicately shimmering light to the room despite the chilly atmosphere. I tried not to look in my father's eyes so that he would not see that I had lied about being ill on his birthday. If he read it in my eyes, he might hit me.

My fear was the same fear I had experienced when I was seven. That day, I sat in the back of his red sports car. We slowly entered a car wash, and my father turned off the engine, waiting for the car to be moved along the conveyer belt to the enormous cleaning brushes. Just as the car wheels rolled onto the conveyer belt and the car was being drawn toward the giant vibrating brushes, my father realized that the trunk was not completely closed.

"Close the trunk!" he screamed. From the backseat, I looked at him with big eyes. I had no idea how to do it. Suddenly, he threw himself into the backseat, landing like a wild animal on top of me, pushing me down. Quickly, he opened the trunk and then closed it properly. I could feel his anger and was terribly afraid that he would hit me. He returned to his seat, bristling with anger. He looked in the rearview mirror with narrowed eyes and said, "You are worthless!" I cowered, not daring to move or speak.

As I sat at my father's ebony table, I had the same feeling of being a failure. Cowering, I grabbed hold of the wooden bench, as if it could give me some protection and stability.

With angry eyes, my father addressed me: "I am deeply disappointed that you did not attend my birthday dinner. I paid your expenses all during your childhood, and you did not even show up for my sixtieth birthday."

I dared to glance at his face. A voice in my head told me, *It is even worse than he thinks: you spent his birthday with the man he hates. You have betrayed him, just as your mother did when she started a love affair with Wolfgang.* I detested myself for my lie. I detested the fact that I hadn't been honest.

My father had not finished talking about his birthday. He said firmly, "That was very wrong of you to be ill on my birthday. The Bible says, 'Honor your father.'" I couldn't remember how often he had said this.

I didn't care what the Bible said. I was out of patience with his expectations. Silently, I asked myself, *But what if I really had been ill? Don't I have the right to be ill?* Aloud, I answered, "I am sorry but I was ill. I really could not come." I hated myself for not standing up for myself. Why hadn't I cut all ties with him, as my sister had done right after my mother's death? What was I looking for? Hadn't I seen enough? I wasn't sure.

I decided to change the subject. I had just landed my first job after college. It was the first money I would earn, and it was exactly the right position for me.

"Papa, I have a job! I'll work as a vendor manager for a mobile telecommunications company. They'll give me the authority to set up my area. And I'll negotiate in English!" I told him with a happy smile. I said silently, *Your daughter is now an industrial engineer, and she has found a job. Please be proud of me; just one time, be proud of me.* How I longed for his appreciation. How I longed for his love. I was a puppy who danced around to get attention from the top dog.

My father looked at me and said, "Just be careful not to be raped in the underground garage of your company at night. People are evil. And even though you have a job now, I expect you to continue visiting me at least every other weekend. That's your duty as my daughter." That was all he said.

Who is this man sitting opposite me? Where did all this negativity come from? How I would have loved to have received his affirmation. Something nice. Was this too much to ask from a father? I did not know. The only comparison I had was Wolfgang, and he was no better. Certainly, it was too much to ask from my father. I knew I had to give up any hope that he'd ever love me. Hope can be a senseless feeling. I sighed. When I was little, my father had doubted that I was his daughter. Sometimes, deep in my heart, I allowed myself to dream that I wasn't his daughter. But if I looked in the mirror, all I saw was that I had the shape of his head, and if I looked at my small hands and stubby fingers, all I saw were his hands. I could not deny that I was his daughter. My blood was his blood. Would I become like him? I feared the answer. I did not ever want to become like my father. I feared my inner demon.

I rejected my father for many years; yet by rejecting my father, I rejected myself. I hated that part of me that came from him. When I saw my hands, I saw his hands. I had inherited 50 percent of his chromosomes, so I feared that I would become like him. I couldn't accept or respect myself just as I was. I lacked self-esteem and trust in myself. I couldn't see any positive traits in myself, so I continued for a long time in an abusive relationship with my father.

I started my new job as a vendor manager some weeks later. The work offered me a safe space, free from the negativity of my past. I got to know my colleagues. At work, nobody knew about my past and my difficult family relations. My success at work helped me to develop self-esteem as a professional, and I began to have some belief in myself.

My maternal grandfather died in January 2000. Two weeks after his death, I visited my father. That weekend he told me, "I am glad that man is dead. It's his fault that my marriage broke up, because he allowed your mother to live in his house when she left me. I am really glad that the old man is dead. For you, your grandfather is dead. You must feel sad. Come, I will hug you." I asked myself whether he would ever forgive anyone. He had not forgiven my mother for divorcing him more than twenty-five years earlier.

Then I remembered what he had said about his older brother after he had died of cancer: "Even though he's dead, I'd love to kick his ass." His words had shocked me. I had never known my uncle, but I knew that he had been an attorney and had worked on cases of child pornography on the Internet. It seemed to me quite a decent job. No, forgiveness was something that did not exist in my father's world.

My father came closer. He waited for a reaction; he wanted me to cry. He opened his arms to embrace me. No, I didn't want to give him the satisfaction. I hid my sadness behind a smile. *Just don't cry. Don't give him any opportunity to touch you. Don't give him any opportunity to violate your mother's family's dignity any longer.* I moved away and said harshly, "No, I am not sad. He was eighty-six and wanted to die. That's life." I lied just to protect my privacy. I hated saying such cold words. But I did not want to show vulnerability in front of my father. I just wanted to protect myself.

The death of my grandfather liberated me from my loyalty to my family. I knew that he wanted me to stay in touch with my father (a man he hated) and my stepfather. Before his death, I never really understood why my grandfather insisted on my maintaining these relationships. Now, I believe that his motivation was to protect the estate. Money and possessions were important to him because he and my grandmother had lost everything during World War II and had to start all over again afterward.

I also believe that money and possessions were so important in my family because they did not believe in something higher: God, the Higher Self, or the Universe. Words such as *soul* or *spirit* were unknown to them, so an estate would be all that was left of them after death. Despite what he said about being a Catholic, even my father did not believe in the soul; only the rules of the Catholic Church—when they seemed to favor him—were of interest to my father.

I recall reading in an article written by a facilitator for family constellations—I can't recall who it was or where the article appeared—that many soldiers returned from the horrors of World War II with a piece missing from their souls. My grandparents did not fight during the war, but they endured many bombings in Berlin. My grandmother fought for her dignity so that the foreign soldiers would not rape her. And my grandfather spent seven years in a former concentration camp, where rape, starvation, and violence were all a part of daily life. I assume that my grandparents lost parts of their souls in the agony that they had experienced and that it just would have been too much for them to face this agony in order to recover what was missing from their souls. I had always seen my grandfather as an old man who had lost the most precious person in his life—his daughter. I wanted to be nice to him. Now, after his death, I didn't have to obey his wishes anymore.

My relationship with Michael was similar to my relationship with my father. We had been together for nearly eight years. He told me regularly that he didn't love me or that I was fat and ugly. We didn't live together or even see each other much. The high points of our relationship were our regular holidays. We had taken at least seven trips to the United States. I had loved our long walks in that country's different national parks. I stayed with him because I didn't know any better. I thought that his behavior was normal. Insulting and unloving behavior was symptomatic of the problems in our relationship.

In May 2000, I sat on my beige carpet and watched TV in my tiny apartment in the heart of Schwabing, just a five-minute walk from the English Garden, a Munich park with old trees and vast areas of grass that in the summer months invited the visitor to lie down and dream. To get there, I had to cross Leopoldstrasse, where I could enjoy coffee at one of the many outdoor cafés and watch the world go by. My one-room apartment had a sofa bed, which I was leaning against, a small marble bistro table with chairs, and a reddish wooden wardrobe. My TV sat on a small table.

The phone rang. I thought that it must be Michael. He had gone on holiday to Lisbon with his friend Martin. The night before, I had come home late and seen my answering machine blinking. When I started the replay, I heard his voice saying, "Hey. We're here. We're going to go out now for dinner, and I'll switch off my mobile."

Hmm. Michael never switches off his mobile, I thought.

Now I got up quickly and answered the phone. "Hello?"

"It's me," Michael responded.

"How is Lisbon?" I had never been there, and I was eager to hear details. I also wanted to keep him involved in a conversation so that I could hear his voice a bit longer. I leaned against the doorway between the living room and the bathroom to stretch a bit. Suddenly, I heard a strange noise in the ceiling, just like a little creek in the Alps.

"Well, quite nice. We went for a short stroll in the city, and now we're going to get ready to go to dinner," Michael said.

Suddenly, a flood of water poured through the ventilation hole in the ceiling of the bathroom. I stared in horror at the water rushing into my bathroom. *Where is it coming from?* Within seconds, the bathroom floor was covered by water. In my imagination, I saw the entire apartment flooded.

"Shit, water is coming through the ventilation hole! What should I do?" I cried.

"I am on holiday now and am not interested in hearing about your problems. I'll call you tomorrow. Bye," he replied and hung up.

I stood there alone in my apartment, trying to figure out a solution to my problem. I had learned to deal with my life alone. I did not expect Michael's help anymore.

That evening, after the flooding had stopped and after I had mopped up the mess in my bathroom, I thought about my phone conversation with Michael. *What can I expect from a partner? What is a relationship? What does a good relationship look like?* All I knew were my mother's relationships. What was her relationship with my father like? She had once commented that she had fallen in love with Wolfgang because he was gentle in bed; my father had been aggressive. But Wolfgang had cheated on her. When he was angry, he hit my sister, who was always fighting for her rights. And once in a while, he hit me when I did not do as I was told.

By contrast, Michael did not hit me. That was much better than at home. Yet was this the best I could do? Love seemed to consist of suffering. Was that really what love was all about? The question seemed too big to answer.

My relationship with Michael was sabotaged by his disinterest, his boredom, and his insults and by my withdrawal. Over the preceding eight years, the relationship had not evolved. We had not established dreams in common. For a year, I had been asking Michael to live with me. He always said that it was not yet the right time. Several times, I had a gut feeling that Michael was lying to me—that he was seeing other women. When I mentioned my suspicion, he said, "You are insane." I didn't know how to react because I didn't have proof. I did not trust my gut feeling. Even though Michael's words hurt, I started to wonder whether he was right.

Some weeks after my telephone discussion with Michael, I did something loving for myself. I decided to get a cat again. After my dying mother had told me that I had failed, I had lost the belief that I could take care of anybody; now, eight years later, I had finally recovered to the extent that I believed that I could take care of a cat. Animals had been my childhood companions, giving me security and comfort and helping me to establish healthy bonds in an unhealthy environment. I decided to get an old cat because I wondered how long I would live. My maternal great-grandmother had died at ninety-one. My grandmother had died at seventy. And my mother had been only fifty when she died. Would I die at thirty? I did not want a kitten because I feared that a kitten would be left alone when I died. Ten-year-old Orlando was a small male cat with nearly yellow eyes, wise-looking like a Sphinx. He instantly loved me and his love helped me to recover.

Then I began jogging. I needed to get stronger. It was rigorous exercise and at first I wasn't certain it was helping. But after some months, I saw progress. I was on my way.

Facing Reality

Due to my increased self-esteem, I was slowly able to face reality. My relationships with my father, Wolfgang, and Michael were horrible. I didn't want to have people like that in my life, and so I withdrew more and more.

Some months after our trip to Thailand, I visited Wolfgang at his home for the first time since our holiday. I wanted to see Mimic. When I entered the house, the dog came toward me. When I saw her, I was shocked. She now was about 20 pounds overweight and could hardly walk. She was not able to put her legs on my shoulders anymore to greet me. She seemed like another dog.

"What happened?" I asked Wolfgang.

"Well, she does not want to get up from the floor if I do not give her treats. So each time I want her to move, I have to give her treats. She does not even want to go for a walk. If I take her out, she just turns around and goes home," he replied innocently.

I looked at him with disgust. So it was the dog's fault that she had eaten too much? Why had he done this to the dog? He was supposed to take care of her. I didn't want to talk to him about Mimic. I felt desperately sad for the dog, and I did not know how to stop Wolfgang from mistreating her.

"How is your relationship with Corinna going?" I asked. He had known Corinna for four years. She was his girlfriend, sort of. She was not beautiful enough for him, so each time Wolfgang found a better-looking woman he would leave her. When the new relationship did not work out, he would return to her.

Corinna tolerated this behavior, but I did not understand why. She seemed to be a very warm-hearted woman.

"Well, we just went for a camping trip together. It was nice. And I invited Sandra to go to a few concerts and operas. Also, in four months, I'll take a trip to Burma with Brigitte."

I looked at him, astonished. He had dated Sandra several times. She was a very good-looking and elegant woman in her fifties. However, he had told me that he did not want to continue with her because she wanted a man who paid the rent on her apartment. He seemed to have changed his mind. And Brigitte was an old friend who pursued him, yet he always rejected her. Like Corinna, Brigitte was not attractive enough to meet Wolfgang's standards.

"Three women? Isn't that a bit much?" I asked myself why these women would accept this arrangement.

"Well, it's perfect for me. They do not know about each other."

I was revolted by his game. I thought about Corinna. Did she really think that he would go to Burma alone? She had known him now for such a long time.

I did not know what to say, so I sat on the floor to pet the dog on her pendant ears; she especially liked this. But when I touched her ear, she yelped.

"Does she always do this?" I asked Wolfgang cautiously.

"Yes, she has been doing it for several weeks. I don't know what happened," he replied disinterestedly.

Why doesn't he look after her? I asked silently as I picked up her ear and looked inside. There was a nasty infection. I had never before seen an infection so bad. "That looks horrible. You have to take her to the veterinarian," I told him. I felt bad because the dog was so neglected. For a moment, I was tempted to take her to my apartment. But she was used to living in a huge house with a garden, and I had a small apartment. And she loved Wolfgang. He was her "top dog." I sighed deeply.

"Really? I had not noticed."

When I drove home that night, I knew that it had been the

last time that I would see my dog. I would not return to Wolfgang's house anymore. I did not want to see him any longer. I could not deal with the way he treated the dog and the games he played with women. He manipulated people. Deep in his heart, he did not care for anybody but himself.

One month later, I received a letter from him. It said that I owned half the dog and so I would have to pay half the veterinary costs. He had included several bills. I decided not to pay them. He was the owner of the dog, and I wanted him to take responsibility for her. He also had much more money than I had. I only feared that one day I might find my dead dog at my door, his last present to me. I felt in my bones that he was capable of such behavior.

I also knew that he hated Anna. When I had resumed contact with Wolfgang, I had wanted to believe that he had attacked Anna after my mother's death because he couldn't cope with his grief over the loss of his beloved wife. I had wanted to think that he had lashed out on impulse.

But years passed and his position remained rigid. He showed no regret about the incident but continually insisted that Anna had acted so badly that he did not want her in his life again—even though he never specified what her failure was.

I now think that he treated Anna and me differently out of calculation: I was submissive and so he considered me easy prey, someone who could be used for his own ends. My sister, on the other hand, he saw as a threat: she inconvenienced him by fighting for her needs.

Further, my sister was with my mother when my mother first discovered Wolfgang's infidelity, so Anna's presence might have been a constant thorn in his side. Of course, Wolfgang would never think to blame himself for our mother's death—never believe that his infidelities could have caused her cancer to return.

I was lucky. He never contacted me again.

My experiences with Wolfgang were painful. But in my healing process, I found that, because Wolfgang was not related to me by blood, my relationship with him was easier to heal and was less important than my relationship with my father, even though I had spent more time with Wolfgang than with my father.

In August 2000, I received a phone call from my father at home. He said, "Natalie, your grandmother has died. I expect you to be at the funeral next Thursday at 4:00 p.m." I had seen my grandmother twice in the preceding twelve years. She was a kind lady, small and fragile with a collapsed spine. She had blonde hair, wore glasses, and spoke in a tremulous voice. My father had been condescending to her. When I listened to his words, I suddenly felt like one of his silver candleholders, his valuable possession, which he would show off, telling the world that it was expensive. I saw myself by his side at the funeral and how he would embrace me to mitigate his pain. The image was unbearable. I knew that he would play his game to show the world that he was a loving father, in possession of a loving daughter. *Loving.* Did he know what the word meant? I had never heard a loving word out of his mouth, never been the recipient of a loving glance.

I felt bad about not paying my grandmother my last respects, but I did not want to play the role of the daughter who supported her beloved father. I was fed up with the masquerade.

Luckily, the funeral was supposed to be during working hours, so I quickly told him, "I'll check my calendar at work and see whether I have meetings that day. I'll let you know."

He said, "I expect you to be there," and hung up.

Two days later, I received a call from an unknown number at work. When I answered, I heard the voice of his wife, Gabriela. She said that it was important to my father that I attend the funeral. I should think about my decision because not to show up would be wrong.

"Your deadline is two days from now. You have to let us know by then," she said and hung up. I had never given my office number to my father or her, so she must have asked the receptionist to put her through. I did not like her invading what I considered to be my sacred space.

Two days later, I was in Michael's living room in the heart of Schwabing, two minutes away from my place. It had black built-in furniture; a blue sofa hugged the wall. Next to the TV was the bronze horse Michael had bought on our most recent holiday in Florida. It was wild, free, and strong. In the shop, a small horse had stood by its side. I had bought that one in the hope that one day the horses would stand together in the apartment that we shared.

Two days had passed. Today, I had to phone my father.

"I'll phone him in an hour," I said to Michael, who was watching TV. He nodded. I knew that it would be a farewell forever. I did not want to see him any longer. I was done with his manipulations. I did not know what to expect after this, but I knew that it would be better. Maybe someday I'd be able to face myself in the mirror and feel a bit of dignity. I was not sure how it would feel. *Dignity.* It was nearly too much to hope for. I sighed. My inner voice told me to be calm. *It's just a phone call. Why do you fear him so much?* I felt a pressure in my throat. *Just one phone call and then it will be over.* I sighed. *The last phone call.* I asked Michael to switch off the TV, went to the phone, and called the number.

"*Hel*-lo," my father said, the syllables slowly drawn out. How well I knew his voice. How much I hated hearing it.

"It's me," I replied.

"Ah, so you will come tomorrow?"

"No, I will not come." I felt relieved. I had really done it. I had said no. He could not ignore me anymore.

"You have to come. She was your grandmother. You have to show her respect."

Naturally, he had found my weak point. I felt guilty and I hoped silently that my grandmother would forgive me. I repeated, "No, I cannot come."

My arms and my hands started to tremble. My knees were jelly. *It's just a phone call. He's not standing in front of me. He can't do anything to me.* Within seconds, my whole body was shaking; I was facing the venom-spitting cobra again, just as in the psychologist's office ten years earlier.

Michael came to my side, touched my shoulder, and looked into my eyes. He gestured that I should finish the call.

My father continued talking, saying something that I did not understand. I just repeated, "No, I will not come tomorrow," and hung up.

Silence. My body was still shaking. I sat down on the sofa. My father would never love me for myself. There was no reason to hope anymore. The game was over. Never again would I have to listen to his lectures. Never again would I allow him to touch me. Tears flowed down my cheeks. I had really done it. I never had to see him again.

Cutting the ties with my father was an important step for me. I believe that I would not have been able to heal if I had continued our relationship. The more distance I put between my father and me, the better able I was to heal. I believe that parents should help their children to grow and to follow their dreams. My father was never willing or able to do this.

In the preceding seven months, my relationships with three people important in my life had come to an abrupt end. More was yet to come.

On a sunny Friday afternoon in November, I sat in my car at the traffic light near Münchner Freiheit (Freedom of Munich, named to honor locals who resisted Hitler), a public square near the English Garden in Schwabing. The light was soft and the temperature was mild while the sun slowly sank. I was in the middle of the usual rush hour traffic jam before turning onto Leopoldstrasse. Suddenly, I spotted Michael's green Ford Fiesta in front of me. We had not seen each other much during the preceding months, even though we lived so near each other. I had been tired of talking to him. But now, I felt a flutter in my heart. I smiled. I had missed this feeling for such a long time. I was looking forward to his call that evening. The traffic light changed and his car took a right turn while I continued driving down Leopoldstrasse. I looked happily at the cafés and shops, made my left turn shortly before the Siegestor, and pulled into my parking spot.

At home, I waited for Michael's call. It had been a long time since I was eager to hear his voice. He did not call. Finally, I lost patience and decided to call him; I knew that he must be at home. I had not done this for weeks.

"Hello?" he answered the phone.

"Hi, it's me. Do you know that I saw you in your car while you were driving home from work? Isn't that funny?" I said to him.

On the other end, there was a moment of silence, and then he said rapidly, "Oh, she is just a colleague. I drove her to the U-Bahn."

There was a subway station right in front of the building where he worked, but I did not say this. I was tired of fighting and arguing, so I just said, "OK, well, let's talk tomorrow," and hung up the phone.

My relationship with Michael was a safe harbor. It was predictable; it was the pain I knew. But during the preceding year, I had gotten fed up with his behavior; often I didn't even care anymore whether he betrayed me. I had withdrawn on an emotional level, so my reaction was boredom. I stayed nine years with him, repeating my mother's example, staying much too long in a relationship that lacked love or appreciation.

Some weeks later, we celebrated New Year's with Michael's friends. We all stood together in front of the Friedensengel, surrounded by a huge crowd. They were about to fill their plastic cups with champagne to toast the New Year.

Somebody screamed, "Happy New Year! Happy 2001!"

Suddenly, the air around me was full of smoke from the fireworks, and I felt a bit deafened by the bangs of the firecrackers. Michael turned around and gave me a brief New Year's kiss. A second later, he had gone over to his friends and was concentrating fully on igniting his fireworks. I looked at him as he moved around, lighting one after the other. He loved New Year's Eve. He was like a little child with shining eyes. He had already forgotten that I was present. I knew him so well. In the past, I would have tried to be closer to him, to receive a hug or two. This year, I did not try anymore. I just stood there, emotionless, trying to cope with the freezing cold of the night.

Another New Year's Eve like this with Michael? Suddenly, I felt a surge of anger. No. I could not cope with another year like this. I had asked him countless times whether he wanted to live with me. He always said that he was not ready. Not ready after nine years? I couldn't accept this excuse any longer. How many times had he told me that he did not love me? Countless times. Each time had left a little mark on my heart. I sighed. How often had he told me that I was fat? Tearfully, I looked down at my body and then at all the slim ladies around me. I'd never be as beautiful as they were. How often had his head swiveled to gaze at a good-looking lady while walking by my side?

Suddenly, I felt lonely. How deep is loneliness if you have a partner? Endless, like an abyss. *Well, my father never loved me, so why should Michael?* My hope that Michael might love me one day had died after I had cut my ties with my father. *A relationship without love isn't worth it. I'd rather be single for the rest of my life than continue in a dead relationship.*

How should I do it? I did not know. He was my first boyfriend. I had nobody. Because I had never experienced secure relationships in my family, I didn't regard the relationship with my sister as a secure one. I had only my work.

It was so difficult for me to leave Michael because I lacked self-esteem. My inner dialogue was painful. I believed that I was ugly, that I was worse than any other person on the planet, and that I was unlovable. I believed all the negative words that Michael said about me. I saw myself as a failure, a loser, partly because I had stayed in an emotionally abusive relationship. I believed Michael's insults and that made it more difficult to leave. I wasn't able to see that I was an attractive and intelligent woman. I wasn't able to see my own beauty, to appreciate myself, and to value my positive attributes. Michael defined my worth; I saw myself through his eyes. My relationship with myself was a distant one. Many times, I did not even like looking at myself. I didn't love myself and I didn't care for myself.

Five weeks later, I trudged up the stairs to my apartment. I knew I had to break up with Michael right away. We had booked a holiday in Nepal some weeks earlier. *Nepal.* It had been a dream for me. I had already read three travel guides. I had wanted this trip to change my life. I had been sure that I would find something special there. Nepal with Michael? My inner voice said no. Nepal was so important to me. I wanted either to go there with the man I wanted to spend my life with or not go at all. Michael was no longer the man I wanted to spend my life with. I had needed him after my mother's death. He had helped me survive. Now it was over. I stood at my apartment door, keys in my hands. What would be the best way to tell him? I didn't know. Later that night, he phoned me.

"I've booked two more nights at The Dwarika's Hotel in Kathmandu," he said. I could hear the pleasure in his voice. He loved traveling. Together, we had visited much of the United States, from the West Coast to the East Coast, from San Diego to Niagara Falls. I did not want to take another trip with him. I had to tell him the truth.

"Michael, we will not go to Nepal together. I am leaving you. I will pay the cancellation fees for the trip," I said calmly. I knew that the phone was not the best way to tell him. But I could not wait any longer. We had not seen each other for two weeks.

"You can't do this to me! You can't cancel these holidays. We have to talk," he replied angrily.

"OK. I'll come over to your place tomorrow after work."

The next evening, I went directly to his place after work. When I rang the bell, he used a buzzer to open the door of the apartment house. I walked up to the third floor. *How often have I climbed these stairs?* I did not know. He stood at the door, waiting for me. Fury showed in his eyes. We went into his living room. I glanced at the bronze horse, symbol of my broken dream of a future with him.

I had needed nine years to realize that our relationship consisted of some nice holidays.

"So you have thought about going to Nepal with me?" I looked into his eyes. *Nine years.* I had hoped that maybe one day he'd love me.

"I will not go to Nepal with you," I said.

"We have taken so many trips together; just go on this holiday with me. You can leave me afterward." We had already played this game once, a year earlier. We had gone to Florida together, even though he wanted to break up; he wanted his freedom. I loved being abroad with him because it gave me the illusion of a connection with him. During our holidays, he did not have anyone else to talk to or hang out with, so I was important to him. The result of this travel was that we continued staying together. I had always wished for a future with him. I was not able to just have sex with a man.

"No, I will not go on holiday with you. It's over." I knew that I had to be tough, even though it was difficult. I knew how much he loved traveling on holiday. He seemed to live to go on holiday.

Suddenly, his expression changed. I knew this mood. The child within was coming out. His mother had told me once that if she refused him anything when he was a child, he would scream and fling his body down, his fists furiously pounding the ground. He would not stop until he got what he wanted. Inside, I smiled when he erupted and said, "You can't do this to me! You know how important my holidays are to me." It was time to leave. Once, during an argument, he had thrown something at me. I did not want that to happen again.

"I'll go now. It's over." I gave him my small bronze horse, once a symbol of my hope for our future, and turned around to leave.

Angrily, he shouted at my back, "It's time for you to come to terms with your father and stepfather!" The words were a dagger in my heart. Never before had he said anything critical about how I dealt with those men. But I knew he was right. I had to get over them. A shadow entered my heart. How should I get over them? How could I cope with the heritage of my father? Would I become as emotionally unwell as he was? I did not know. When would I finally know? The burden of sharing my father's blood weighed heavily on me.

When I crossed the street to go to my car, I heard the scratchy noise of a window opening and Michael's voice shouting something. The wind carried away his words. For a moment, I thought how wonderful it would have been if he had felt the same passion for me as he felt for his holidays. Deep inside, I had never expected him to love me. Who would love me? I was an ugly duckling, a short, plain woman with eyes full of sadness, a victim who would never win. Who would ever be able to love me? In the end, what were love and relationships all about? Suffering and loss. Alone in my inner world, I went home.

When I gave up the hope that my father would ever love me, I started an inner process to finally accept that Michael would never love me. I began to understand that a relationship should consist of two people loving each other while loving themselves.

After I left Michael, I was able to tell my sister my secret while she was on a visit in Munich. Our relationship had improved after the death of our grandfather. We were together in my apartment on a Thursday night. She was sitting on my sofa, and I stood next to the cat tree. It was already dark outside. I wanted to talk to her about the sexual abuse. It was time that I shared my secret with her. My body felt tense. At some point, I had to start. So I just started.

"I need to tell you something. I was sexually abused when I was a small child, about three. It happened only once." A voice in my head said angrily, *Why does this bother you so much? Don't make a mountain out of a molehill. It happened only once.* Yet I felt how a high, invisible wall separated me from my sister. I wanted to reach out to her. I couldn't. *Maybe you can break through the wall?* I looked at her entreatingly. *It is so lonely here behind my wall; darkness and emptiness surround me.*

I rubbed my arm. It had been difficult to tell my sister the truth. Then I told my sister another secret. I was engaging in self-harm in moments when my inner pain became so big that I shut down all feelings. In those moments, I used my fist to bang on my left arm until it was black and blue. I knew that hurting myself was unhealthy. I just could not stop. Michael had called me insane when he saw me do it once. I had never known how to deal with it. *What does Anna think? Does she believe me? Why can't I just stop?*

Anna looked distressed but not surprised; it was just another piece of the puzzle of our childhoods. "What happened to you was horrible! And you really don't know who it was? There were only four men in our lives: our father, our grandfather, Wolfgang's father, and Wolfgang." Her eyes were full of worry. I shook my head. I didn't know who it was—it could have been any man, even a stranger—and I didn't want to talk about it. I had said what I wanted to say. I wanted to be normal. I petted my cat. Feeling the warmth of his fur gave me comfort.

That day, I started to accept the sexual abuse as part of my reality. Until then, I hadn't been able to share it with anybody; it had been just too much for me. In my relationship with Michael, I had been almost completely unable to connect with my body. I had felt numb because I had shut down feelings and body sensations to a great extent after the sexual abuse. When I started to accept the fact of the abuse, the feelings and sensations in my body began to wake up, even though it was a process that took many years to be complete.

To this day, I have not remembered the identity of the person who abused me. This lack of knowledge has not been relevant to my healing or to my life.

At the time that I shared my secret with Anna, I still wasn't able to visit a therapist, because my family had given me a very unfavorable impression of therapists, which still blocked me.

My father was a trainer for leadership development. He wasn't a therapist, but he had studied Freud and had used Freudian theories to manipulate me as a child. In my eyes—despite the kindness of Laura, the therapist I had visited once when my mother was dying—therapists were just like my father. And even though my mother had sent me to Laura, she and her family usually judged people who needed therapy as insane. Members of my mother's generation were not accustomed to asking for emotional help. It took me many years to discover that, as in every profession, there are good therapists and bad therapists, and that any psychological tool or theory can be used in a respectful, supportive way or in a manipulative way. Once I was able to let go of my prejudice and think of a therapist or coach as somebody who wanted to help me, I was able to achieve profound changes in my life. But at that stage, I was not yet ready for this.

After I broke up with Michael, my personal life suffered. I was stuck with the belief of my family of origin: the family and the partner was the only social circle a person had in life. When I lost Michael, I lost my social life.

The only social contact I had was my work, but I couldn't

work every day. The dark night of my soul occurred on Ascension Day, a national holiday in Germany. It was a warm, sunny day in the summer, the sky was amazingly blue, and the usual noise of drivers going to work or going home or desperately looking for a parking spot was absent. The sounds of children's voices drifted into my apartment, full of excitement about going to play in the English Garden. Beams of sunlight entered my apartment.

Orlando sat on his cat tree, Sphinx-like. He hadn't moved for hours. He just sat there and did not move his eyes from me. I sat on the floor, my legs stretched out on the floor, my back leaning against the sofa. I was motionless. My left arm had blue spots. The hurt didn't help anymore. I felt only emptiness. *What is life all about?* I felt nothing. I was nothing. I was worthless. *Why was I born? What else can I expect?* I could not continue like this any longer. Life was pain and darkness. I was worthless. I was unlovable.

I thought about my options. I could slit my wrists in the bathroom. *But how would Anna feel when she found out? It would be horrible for her. And Orlando? How long would it take for somebody to find him? Maybe he would starve.*

I looked at him and saw him sitting on his tree. Normally, he sat in my lap when I was home. I looked into his wise eyes as he sat there, just observing me. I had the impression that he said, *Please don't give up*, but that he knew I had to make the decision for myself. *How can I find a way to live with all my pain? Am I any good?* I could not feel it. *How can I cope with all the darkness inside me? How can I live as an outcast of society? How can I live with this dark, overwhelming, and horrifying secret? How can I live without connecting to anybody?* I felt so numb that I could not even cry anymore.

No, suicide was not possible. I did not want to burden my sister with my death, and I did not want to betray Orlando. I looked out the window and saw the wonderfully blue sky. I sat in my invisible prison. No way to break out; the walls were too thick. I longed so much to be part of life outside and I knew I wasn't.

A thought crossed my mind. The mental hospital. *That's the solution!* It was a flash of lightning. *I can ask to be admitted to the mental hospital. I'll be protected there for the rest of my life. It is where I belong. I am insane.* I sighed. That was an option. In slow motion, I got the phone book from the shelf, and I got my phone and looked up the number. I put the open page that showed the phone number in front of me and held the receiver in my hand. I did not have the strength to call.

I looked at Orlando again. *I'm sorry, I can't take you with me,* I told him silently. He observed me. His previous owner had told me that she had tried to give him away several times, but it had not worked out because he became furious and attacked the person. He did not like many people. But when he moved in with me, he started to sit on my lap after three days. He was always waiting for me at the door when I came home, and he followed me around, somehow telling me in his language what had happened during his day. He would not stop following me until I sat down and he was able to lie on my lap. I looked at him. *I'm sorry that I can't keep you,* I told him silently. I felt like he answered, *It's your choice.* I sighed. I looked at the phone book in front of me and at Orlando.

Suddenly, the shriek of my phone broke through the thick silence in the room. Once. Twice. I was not able to answer. The answering machine started running.

"Hi, this is Martin. I just wanted to know how you are. Call me." A touch of warmth entered my apartment. Martin was Michael's best friend. I had not expected him to contact me after I broke up with Michael. Again, I looked at the phone book in front of me and then at Orlando. The sun shone more brightly through the window behind his cat tree. The voices on the street seemed closer. Very slowly, the cloud of darkness that surrounded me cleared a bit. Maybe there was another option.

I remembered a conversation at work three months earlier.

It had been late in the evening. Most of the desks were empty; people had left for home. Only my colleague Silke, a tall woman who sat next to me, and I were not able to leave work. We started to talk about our childhoods, and Silke said, "When my parents separated, I stayed with my mother, but I always had a wonderful relationship with my father. I know that I can trust him, and that he would do anything for me." Her voice was full of love. I felt that trust must be something special, and I became aware that I did not know how it felt to trust my parents. I had never thought about trusting them.

What does it feel like to trust your father? I asked myself. Then I asked Silke the same question.

She gave me an astonished look and said, "Well, it is the same unquestioning trust that a baby has with her mother, knowing that she will always be protected, that this bond will never break."

I looked at her. No, I had never known this feeling toward my parents. I became aware that I lacked trust, and I asked myself what it would feel like to trust others, even if just for a moment.

Now it seemed that Martin had friendly feelings for me. Otherwise, he would not phone me. Maybe there was another option: I could trust other people. Maybe this would improve my situation. I looked at Orlando. Maybe it was worth it. I could give it a try, and maybe my life would make more sense. I had nothing to lose. I stayed that night on the carpet, exhausted and unable to move.

The next day, I was ready to phone Martin. "Hi, Martin, it's me, Natalie," I said when he answered the call.

"Hi! Nice to hear from you. How are you?" he said. He sounded happy to hear from me. I had never known what he thought of me.

"Not so well. I'd like somebody to talk to. Would you have time to take a walk?" I asked cautiously. How would he respond? I needed to get out of the apartment. I had to see somebody.

"Sure. How about going to the English Garden?" he asked me. I sighed with relief. Martin made it really easy for me.

When he rang the bell some hours later, I went downstairs. When I left the house, the sun hit my eyes. It was shining so brightly. He gave me a hug, and we started walking down Georgenstrasse toward the English Garden. I suddenly felt the warmth of the sun on my skin. It was comforting.

"So what is going on?" he asked me. I looked at him. What part of the truth should I tell him? What part of the truth could he cope with? I decided to stick to the easiest one.

"I feel so lonely. I can't cope with the separation from Michael," I told him. More was not possible. I could not tell him about the sexual abuse or my self-harming behavior. I did not want to shock him. It was too much for me, and I feared that it would be too much for him.

"I understand. If you need me, I'll be there for you. Don't worry about Michael; I can separate my friendship with you from my friendship with him," he said. I felt that he was honest with me. After the death of my mother, when I had been without a home, I lived for two weeks with Martin because I couldn't stay with Cornelia's family for long; they didn't have enough space. Martin had always been kind to me. I was grateful for his offer. I asked him how Michael was and he replied softly, "He's fine. He is dating Tina. She objects to his behavior more than you ever did."

I nodded. Tina was the woman who had been with him in his car that Friday afternoon. He had gone on holiday with her four weeks after I had left him. Suddenly, I needed to clarify something and said, "I have a question about Michael. When you were in Lisbon together, what did you two do at night?" I had to ask this. Michael and I had had many discussions about other women because I had always felt that he was betraying me. When I had mentioned my feelings, he had always attacked me verbally. "You are insane," he had said many times. With all my self-doubts and lack of self-esteem, I had been more than willing to believe him.

"We met two female flight attendants on the plane. We asked

them out for dinner," Martin replied briefly. I did not need more information because it did not matter to me. What mattered was that my gut feeling had been right. I was not so insane. Martin's honesty was a relief.

We continued walking and my legs slowly felt stronger. My mother had never had friends. I had always believed that in life, only the family and the partner could be important. I could not imagine that a friend could give you much attention, appreciation, or affection. My only friend, Cornelia, had moved away from Munich, and at that point we did not communicate much and saw each other even less; years later, Cornelia and I became close. Now I noticed that I had a friend by my side who cared about me. There was an option to continue living. Maybe there was the possibility that I could learn to trust friends. At least, I had to give it a try. I had nothing to lose and everything to gain.

I don't know what would have happened to me if Martin had not called. He phoned at the right time, and I am grateful that he did. As a child, I had learned that I couldn't trust anybody. This belief isolated me. My conversation with Silke opened my eyes because I became aware of my negative conditioning. My decision to learn to trust people was the first important step I took toward healing. It was the foundation of all that came afterward.

In the following months, I got to know some of my work acquaintances better and started to develop a circle of friends.

After I broke off contact with my father, he continued to send me letters and postcards. Sometimes they were written by an apparently loving father who cared for his daughter. And sometimes they were full of manipulation and insults to my mother, my mother's family, and me. Once he sent me the book *Parental Alienation and Parental Alienation Disorder: A Serious Form of Emotional Abuse of Children*. He regarded this book as proof that my alienation from him was my mother's fault. I read the complete book. He had highlighted in yellow the sentences that had drawn his attention. I attributed the described behaviors more to my father than to my mother.

Some years later, I moved and applied to the police for a secret address because I desperately wanted to put an end to receiving my father's unwanted letters. They saw the amount of letters and agreed. When he found out that I had moved, he started to send his letters to my office. After I changed positions at this company, I had Silke send a letter back to his address with a note that I wasn't working anymore at the company. Some weeks later, I received a phone call at the office, which had been put through by the receptionist. I answered and the caller hung up. A week later, his letters started again; he no longer put a return address on them.

Then I changed employers and hoped that his letters would stop. But after two years, I received a message from the company that he was still sending me letters, so I agreed that they could send them to me.

Every End Is a New Beginning

After the end of my relationship with Michael, I expected to stay single for the rest of my life. Yet half a year later, when I had just found some friends, I became increasingly aware of Paolo, a colleague. He was Italian, about six feet tall, with dark, curly hair and brown eyes. He wore a lonely rider leather motorcycle jacket and drove a fourteen-year-old white car so tiny that it seemed too small for him. During the preceding months we had worked together closely, discussing strategies and preparing presentations.

On a sunny day in July, we went out for dinner with Silke and my manager. We entered a typical Bavarian *biergarten* and sat at a table in a wonderful restaurant garden with huge, old chestnut trees. The rays of the evening sun shone softly through the leaves and warmed my skin. Paolo sat opposite me and ate chicken wings. As he ate, I heard a noise like bones cracking. I looked up from my salad. It seemed to be coming from Paolo, so I asked him, "What are you doing?"

He looked up into my eyes and answered, completely calmly, "I eat the gristle. I always do this," and continued eating.

Even though I was a vegetarian, I had to smile. *How sweet*, I thought. That day, we left the restaurant together, and I noticed that our shoulders were almost touching. I appreciated feeling him so close to me. I knew that I was about to fall in love because normally I did not like a man to be so close to me. Deep inside, I was afraid of any man.

Days later, Paolo left to visit his Italian parents and some friends in Mannheim. I missed him and found an excuse to call him. We talked for an hour on the phone. The next Sunday night, I received his text message: "Do you want to go to dinner tomorrow after work?" My heart was jumping for joy.

"Yes, I'd love to," I replied.

The next evening, we went out for dinner at a restaurant close to his apartment. Even though I liked being with him, I felt awkward. It was my first real date with a man—the first time a man had asked to spend time with me, just the two of us. After dinner, he walked me to my car. I knew that he wanted to kiss me, but I knew that I just couldn't. Kissing a man frightened me. And kissing a man for the first time terrified me. For me, kissing was an intimate act, maybe even more intimate than having sex. It was my surrender to a man. *Surrender to a man.* A horrible thought for the part of me that had decided long ago to never again be hurt by a man. The part of me that believed that being in love meant being vulnerable, risking that I'd be hurt again, losing control. That part of me became alarmed.

Paolo's face came close to mine. I panicked. His lips were just inches from mine. I thought that a normal woman would give him a kiss now, and I forced myself to stay. I had heard stories about women kissing strangers at parties. Then it hit me that I couldn't be that normal. Suddenly, Paolo became my enemy, and I dived beneath his arms, opened my car door, and flung myself into my car seat. "See you tomorrow!" I said while I banged my car door shut. While I drove away, I risked a look into the rearview mirror. Paolo was standing in the middle of the road, his arms hanging down helplessly from his shoulders. His face wore a confused expression.

Shit. I had messed it up. What was he thinking about me? Why couldn't I just be like other women? Why was falling in love such a pressure? On the one hand, I wished that I never had to see him again. On the other hand, I longed to have a relationship with him. My body was torn apart. My mind was torn apart. How could I overcome my inner conflict? I did not know.

The next day at work, I ignored Paolo. Late in the afternoon, he came to my desk and said in a low voice, "I don't know what happened yesterday, but maybe we should talk about it. Tonight at my apartment?" I agreed. I knew that I had to see him again to learn about myself and about my life. I didn't find many men attractive, and I didn't want my past to control me.

That evening, I sat next to him on the sofa in his apartment. MTV was playing "When It's Over" ("When it's over / That's the time I fall in love again"). I sat close to Paolo, and he had an arm around my shoulder. Was Michael really over? I feared a repetition. What if Paolo wouldn't love me? If I didn't try, I would never find out. I knew that it was the moment when normal people would kiss. It looked so easy in the movies when other people did it. How I would have loved to kiss Paolo and just be able to enjoy it.

But I felt the presence of my invisible companions. The shadow of my father sat by my right side, huge and mighty as always. It whispered in my head, *No way. There is no way that a man will ever love you.* And there was this tiny, angry monster that was sexual abuse at my left side. *Never,* it said, *never allow a man to touch you. It is dangerous. He will kill you.* As I sat in the middle between the two of them, I felt so vulnerable and confused. I looked at Paolo, feeling ashamed and angry. I was in love with him. Did he know anything of my inner conflicts? I tried to read his eyes. He just sat there. He seemed not to know what to do, not to have the least idea what was going on inside me. And I was not able to communicate it. Shouldn't it be a romantic moment? I longed to kiss him without reservation, the way any normal woman would. I knew I couldn't. I sighed and told myself, *Just close your eyes and jump. If you do it, once it is done you can repeat it. Waiting won't make it easier. It is normal to kiss a man and have sex with him.*

So I locked up my feelings and kissed Paolo. I wanted to be

normal. And then, after I had taken the first step, I forced myself to have sex with him. I connected with my inner prostitute, the woman who pleased a man but would never be intimate with him. I numbed myself and became the whore, who gave pleasure but never allowed herself to receive it.

The next morning, when I left Paolo's apartment at dawn to go home to Orlando, I felt dirty. Deep inside, I knew that it had happened too early and too fast. But at least I had done it.

When I got together with Paolo, I still wasn't able to handle my past. I did what I believed was normal and what I believed society expected from me. I couldn't connect with my own inner voice. I was deeply horrified by the notion of allowing a man to have an intimate relationship with me. I was buffeted about by my own contradictory inner voices and emotions. One part of me yearned to have a relationship; the other part wanted to run away. I believe that I would never have managed to enter a relationship with Paolo if we hadn't worked together. Because I knew that I'd see him again at work, I knew that I couldn't escape him. Being intimate with a man was a threat to me, and I couldn't control my fear. I spent a few nights on his kitchen floor, crying due to my fear. I needed nine more years to finally begin to heal.

My fears took control one Saturday, about a month after we had become a couple. I sat on Paolo's bed, and he stood in front of me. Behind his broad shoulders, I saw the dark green leaves on the tops of the trees in the courtyard of his apartment house complex. In front of the glass doors stood a beige leather sofa and two huge chairs. Kylie Minogue's "Can't Get You Out of My Head" played on the radio. Inside me, there was this angry voice saying that the relationship would never work and that I would get hurt again. With tears in my eyes, I spit out, "An Italian idiot has turned my life into chaos!" I was furious that he had entered my life and that I had fallen in love with him. The moment I spoke, the anger vanished, and I was overwhelmed by sadness. The part that longed to have a relationship had taken control of me again. The fact that I could not avoid seeing him at work made me feel as though I were in a mousetrap. *Why did I choose a colleague?* I asked myself. *Because if you're not forced to interact with a man closely, you don't. You always run away,* was the silent answer.

Paolo looked bewildered. "I'm going to take a shower," he said and went into the bathroom.

My thoughts went wild. *He'll leave you now. You'll end up all alone, and you'll be alone the rest of your life. Why can't you behave like any normal woman? You're worthless.* Tears ran down my face. I was the ball in the game between my competing thoughts.

Minutes later, Paolo returned from the bathroom. His dark hair was still wet, and some drops fell on his shoulders. Quietly, he walked to the bed and stood in front of me. He looked in my eyes and said firmly, "Dummkopf, not idiot. Dummkopf." I couldn't help but smile a little.

Then he asked me what I wanted to do, and I said that I'd like to go for a walk. We went outside and walked down the road some minutes until we arrived at the west bank of the Isar, the river that flows down from the Karwendel Mountains and through Munich. We crossed the Thalkirchner Bridge with its red wooden framework and reached the east bank of the Isar, where the Hellabrunn Zoo was on the right side. The air was filled with the smell of the animals and the straw at the zoo. We turned left and walked into the forest of big trees at the Flaucher, Munich's recreational area in the floodplains of the Isar. The banks were crowded with people who had spent the day sunbathing and were now preparing their barbecue.

Paolo put an arm around my shoulder, and we just walked, hardly speaking. I slowly relaxed. It seemed that he did not want to leave me. I shyly looked at the man by my side. I saw his dark hair and dark eyes. How good-looking he was. Maybe I'd achieve all I longed for; maybe he was the man I was supposed to spend my life with. A small spark of hope flared up. Walking silently by his side, I decided to cancel my plans to move to the United States and to cancel a trip to India that I had planned with Martin. I wanted to give our relationship a chance. This time, I did not want to mess it up.

After six months, I had managed to work through my contradictory feelings about Paolo. I had come to understand that he was different from my father or Michael. I had started to trust him to the extent that my urgent wish to leave him had disappeared. Now I was thrilled to have Paolo in my life.

My routine was the same each day: I stayed at his apartment overnight. Then I got up at 5:30 a.m. to take care of Orlando. I had a bad conscience about leaving him alone so often. When Paolo would visit his parents for a weekend, I enjoyed my time alone. These weekends gave me the distance I needed but only for a short time. Later, I learned that I needed to allow myself a dance between distance and closeness to really deeply connect with a partner. At that time, I wasn't aware of my need.

Nearly ten months later, I decided that I wanted to buy an apartment and to ask Paolo whether he wanted to live with me. I was weary of getting up so early each morning. With Silke accompanying me, I started looking for an apartment. I found a wonderful attic apartment that was still under construction but looked as though it would be full of light due to its high windows.

On a Saturday in May, I sat on the bed in Paolo's apartment and asked him directly, "If I buy this apartment, will you move in with me?"

He looked at me for a moment and replied, "Sure, why not." I felt relieved. He really wanted to live with me. After my painful struggle with Michael, I could hardly believe it.

"Well, the apartment should be ready in August next year,

but I have to start paying on the loan now. I can't afford to pay the loan and pay the rent on my apartment." I felt awkward. It was difficult for me to ask for something. I wasn't used to it.

"You can buy it and then move into my apartment until the other one is ready."

I was happy. He really did want to live with me! Then I addressed the last point on my list: "So if we live together, you will pay half the rent, won't you?"

He looked at me and this time it was not a pleasant look. "Pay half the rent? You're crazy! You'll get money from me, and you'll be the owner of the house. I will not help you pay back your loan," he said firmly.

My stomach hurt. It did not feel right. Much of the money I had to pay was the interest on the loan. I would never get it back. I looked at him. He ignored me. In that moment, I did not start a discussion because I was afraid of conflict. I just decided silently that I would finance the apartment by myself. This would also mean that I would not be financially dependent on him. I remembered my father's phrase, "I paid your expenses all during your childhood." And the unspoken corollary: *And now you have to be here for me.* Even though my inner voice told me that this was wrong, my mind convinced me that it would be much better if I paid for everything myself. That way, Paolo would never have any right to tell me what to do.

This was the first time in my relationship with Paolo that I compromised my values and didn't respect my limits. This led to an imbalance in giving and receiving. His unwillingness to pay half the rent helped me keep one foot outside the relationship. In the months that followed, I started to move my belongings into Paolo's apartment. I would discover later that he followed the changes that were taking place in his apartment with distrust. Deep inside, neither one of us was ready to take this step.

At the end of September, I moved the last of my belongings,

Orlando, and myself into Paolo's apartment. Some of my furniture wouldn't fit into Paolo's apartment, so I had put it in storage. Paolo wasn't at home when I moved my cat in. Orlando immediately began to cautiously explore his new home. That night, Paolo came home. He had spent the evening at Oktoberfest. He was drunk when he staggered into the room. Orlando saw him and fled into the kitchen. He hardly knew Paolo because he had visited my apartment only twice during the preceding year. Paolo followed him and reached out with his arms to catch him, like a baby trying to catch a bird. Paolo was a big man, and I knew that the situation would not end well. I tried to hold Paolo back but failed. When Paolo approached Orlando, it was too much for the cat. He humped his back, hissed, and tried to scratch Paolo. Then he disappeared into the bathroom. Paolo sat on the ground like a disappointed child who had lost his toy.

Throughout the next year, they fought like cats and dogs. Each Sunday morning, Orlando would get up at 5:00 a.m. and saunter coolly to the stereo. He would slowly lift his paw and start to scratch the fiber of the speaker cover. He did it with just one claw, but that was enough. Paolo would sleepily roll out of bed and try to catch him. "Stupid cat," he would mutter. By the time Paolo reached the stereo, Orlando would be hiding out in the bathroom. I was amused by this game. For me, the stereo was just a thing, not as important as my cat. For Paolo, it was serious, and the box was more important than the cat. We never found a resolution of this conflict. Paolo became more and more stressed about my relaxed way of looking at the cat's damage. I did not understand his anger.

One year later, we moved into the newly constructed attic apartment that I had bought. It was open and filled with light. Finally, I had all my furniture in my place. When I moved Orlando into the new apartment, he explored all the furniture with curiosity. He was very ill at that stage. He had feline acquired immune deficiency syndrome (FAIDS), and his liver had stopped working properly, so he sat in front of my wardrobe and meowed. I lifted him into the different compartments where he had once slept. Before, we had lived together in a one-room apartment. Now I had provided him with a new, more spacious home, and I smiled as I observed him explore it.

Two weeks after the move, Orlando's illness worsened, and I had to make the decision to put him to sleep. It was the decision I had feared since he had received the diagnosis of a deadly illness. Once I made the sad choice, I sat in the new apartment with Paolo by my side while I held Orlando. Suddenly, I saw a tear course down Paolo's face. It gave me a special sense of connection with him. A veterinarian came to our home to administer the drug to Orlando. Before he left, he said that he had expected my call much sooner and that it was a miracle that Orlando had survived such a long time with his illness. I saw this as a sign that Orlando enjoyed being with me, and even though I was desperately sad about his death, I felt grateful that he had spent three years with me.

In the days that followed, I would return home in the evening but Orlando was not there to greet me anymore. It was a wonderful apartment, yet without my feline companion, it felt lonely and lifeless. One night, I asked Paolo, "Would you mind if we got cats again? We could get two kittens, and you could teach them not to scratch the stereo."

He looked at me and said, "Yes, we can get kittens." I was relieved.

Four weeks later, two little bundles of gray wool, Thor and Loki, moved into the apartment. They were brother and sister. Thor was really anxious and looked like a shocked owl. Loki gathered up her courage and started to explore the apartment, and Thor ran after her because he was afraid to be alone. I hoped that Paolo would enjoy living with the cats.

Too Afraid to Look

The sexual violence I had experienced influenced my relationship with Paolo. It was impossible for me to have sex with him without shutting down my feelings. I didn't know how Paolo felt about this. Sometimes I had flashbacks about the abuse, mostly during or right after having sex, as on one particular Saturday morning in May 2004. Because I did not experience them in my relationship with Michael, I think that these flashbacks were part of my healing process and my growing intimacy with my own body.

Paolo was holding me tightly in bed after sex. Suddenly, pictures of the abuse came up in my mind again. I cried out, pushed his arms away, and withdrew to my side of the bed, where I cowered in a fetal position. I cried. I couldn't allow him to touch me. Paolo tried to hold me. I said, "Please, just give me some moments alone." I didn't want to hurt him. My reaction had nothing to do with him. I felt his despair. He did not say anything, just remained silent. After ten minutes, I was able to open up again. Silently, I allowed him to hug me. Paolo stayed silent but I knew he felt rejected.

During our relationship, we were not able to communicate openly about the effects of the abuse and what feelings this generated. It was a dark zone in our relationship, which we never talked about. I had informed him about the sexual abuse right at the beginning of our relationship, but he never said anything regarding his feelings and thoughts about this. I myself did not know how to deal with this subject. I had grown up in a family here nobody talked about feelings, so I didn't have a way to communicate properly. The abuse remained a silent obstacle.

I became interested in the subject of abuse and started to read books on how to heal from it. In summer 2004, we spent our holiday in Rome. We were lying on the bed in our wonderful room, which was situated in one of Rome's impressive old palaces. The building had rough stone walls, which were painted a stark white. Reddish ceramic tiles covered the floor, an old dark wooden wardrobe stood against one wall, and a wooden sideboard with a mirror stood near the bed. The windows next to the wardrobe were open, but the wooden blinds were closed, so that only the dimmed light of the sun entered. It was lunchtime and it seemed that the whole city was sleeping, yet sometimes the silence was broken by the noise of a scooter on the road. Paolo lay next to me on the bed, asleep.

I was fully awake, reading my new book, *Was die Seele krank macht und was sie heilt* (*What Makes the Soul Ill and What It Heals*) by Thomas Schaefer. It was about Bert Hellinger, a person I had never heard of before, and his work with family constellation therapy. The book explained that the world a person experiences is shaped by his or her first learning and conditioning, gained through family relationships, and it discussed the hidden dynamics of these relationships. In my case, my family had not been a source of support and protection, helping me to see the world as a happy and safe place, but a source of suffering, which made me see the world as a dark and hostile place.

According to the book, constellation therapy could change a participant's perspective. In a constellation, a participant chooses representatives of his or her family members from among a group of participants and places them in the middle of the group. The constellation facilitator helps the participant recognize his or her own family situation and then guides the constellation process, using healing phrases or movements to help the participant find a new image of his or her family, which aids in resolving obstacles and disruptions in the participant's life. In this way, the participant is helped to reconcile with his or her own destiny, accept his or her place in the family system, and express genuine love for and awareness of his or her family.

The process sounded good. But could it work for me?

When I had seen the book in the bookstore, I had known instantly that I wanted to read it. The title had given me hope: might there be a way to heal my own ill soul? Now I devoured the book, each page revealing to me a new perspective on life that felt right for me. The beauty of Rome was dwarfed by the revelations of the book. It seemed to me that my eyes were as radiant as the eyes of a child who waited for Santa Claus. I read the chapter about sexual abuse. It was so important to me that I had to share it with Paolo. So I said, "Paolo, look what he says here."

Paolo woke with a start and looked at me. I could see in his eyes that something was wrong. He said, "Stop reading that crap. I don't want to hear about it. I want you to spend your time with me, not read about that stuff."

I was puzzled that he was not interested at all and that he had gotten angry with me for trying to become a healthy person. My feelings were not hurt by his reaction. My interest in the subject was based on my own experiences, and I could not expect him to feel the same. But I couldn't stop reading the book. I just stopped sharing my thoughts.

Paolo and I never found a good way to look at the sexual abuse, and we never talked about it openly—our feelings about it, our thoughts about it, or the influence it had on our own relationship. He wanted to delete it from my history, and I couldn't do it. During our relationship, I still looked at the sexual abuse with horror. Paolo stood helplessly on the sidelines and didn't know what to do. After we broke up, we talked about it, and he mentioned that he had always felt responsible for saving me. But I never expected him to fix me. I knew that this was my responsibility.

Our relationship continued. We spent our lives together, went on holidays, went to the movies, and spent weekends in Mannheim with his friends and family. We had our routine. I thought that was what a relationship was all about; I didn't know any other model of a relationship.

Tell Me, Where Have Our Dreams Gone?

One evening in June 2007, I entered a hair stylist's shop. It was on the first floor of an old house at the Sendlinger Tor, one of Munich's historical city gates. I stood at the entrance, overwhelmed by the many hair stylists who ran around busily. I smelled the comforting perfumes of the shampoos in the air. Music was playing quietly. I looked around to see if somebody noticed my presence. The women in the room all looked so beautiful. I felt that I didn't belong with them. A slender woman with long brown hair approached me and said, "Hello. Do you have an appointment?"

"Yes, I am Natalie. I have an appointment at 7:00 p.m."
She looked in her appointment book, nodded, and said that I should follow her. She crossed the huge room, whose walls had green palm leaves painted on them. The room looked a bit like a jungle. On the left side were huge windows that opened to the street. She stopped in front of a seat and indicated that I should sit down and wait.

I sat down in front of a huge mirror, which reflected parts of the opposite side of the room. I looked at myself in the mirror and saw a gray duck with brown hair. She did not have anything special. She was so desperate and life was so boring. Over the past few years, I had grown my hair long. It now hung to the middle of my back. Paolo liked me with long hair. It had never been so long before. Yet it lacked movement; it lacked change. I felt like a slave or maybe a mental patient, stuck in a straitjacket.

For a few months now, I had been losing lots of hair. But that was only one exterior sign of my interior struggle: Each time I washed my hair, I asked myself whether I could justify using the amount of water I had to use to wash it. The world lacked an adequate amount of water. Was my hair really worth using all that water to get it clean? My soul said, *It's not that you ruin nature when you wash your hair. It's that you do not see a purpose to your life. You must give your life a purpose.*

Everything seemed to be dark around me. I could not see any light shining in the darkness. I asked myself what was going wrong. I was thirty-five years old, I had a new job as a product manager with a different company, and I was about to set up a new department. I earned good money. I had a relationship. Yet inside I felt lonely and empty. Sometimes I heard the voice of society: *Buy more. Then you will feel happier.* I had tried this but it hadn't worked out. On the contrary, I had felt even more depressed because I didn't believe this attitude was feasible or sustainable. Was it possible that each generation was supposed to consume more and more? My mind said no, this was not reasonable for humanity or for nature. Each time I washed my hair, I saw my life going down the drain, just like the water. I needed something different, something that could make me see the point of living.

I needed a change. And I would start with my hair. As a child, I had always liked my short hair. I shyly glanced in the mirror. What could I expect of the cut? What would my hair stylist be like? What if she gave me a haircut that looked worse than now? I told myself to be calm: *Don't worry. It can't be worse.*

Suddenly, a woman appeared behind me. She was small and slender, maybe in her fifties, and had red and yellow hair. Her hair seemed to go in every direction. She wore vivid, softly draping Indian-style pants. Had she just left an ashram? For a moment, I was scared. She seemed so different from any other hair stylist I had met. I thought about leaving but I stayed. "What do you want?" she asked.

Looking into the mirror, I said, "I want to cut my hair short. For some months I have been losing hair, and I need a change." She touched my hair, which was bound into a ponytail. "You are right." Suddenly, she had a huge pair of scissors in her hands. In the next moment, she cut my hair, just above the hair tie. She threw the ponytail to the ground. Eight inches of my hair was gone.

My mouth was slightly open—I hadn't expected her to be so fast.

Then she continued touching my hair and said, "Your hair wants to move freely. It is trapped right now. You need more creativity in your life. You are stuck in a life that is not yours."

I looked at her in the mirror. Could this be real? A hair stylist who did not know anything about me was telling me the truth about my life? One part of me was scared. The other part was happy. Finally, somebody from the outside world was confirming what I had heard years earlier. A tiny voice had whispered to me, *Natalie, you need more creativity. I want you to draw again. I want you to express myself.* I had ignored the voice because I had thought that somehow it wasn't appropriate for an adult to draw. My mother hadn't pursued art either.

Now I sat in the chair and thought about my life. Every day was the same: I got up in the morning, went to work, came home again, ate dinner, and watched TV. Paolo and I had even started to watch a cooking show daily. Each evening, we sat silently in front of the TV and watched how the people on the screen lovingly prepared a delicious dinner and then sat together and talked about life. Sometimes I asked myself whether the people on the screen were more real than the two of us. Was this all there was to life? Would this routine continue until the day I died? A shudder ran down my spine. No, I definitely needed a change. I did not want to continue like this.

My hair stylist continued talking. She talked about the Universe and angels. I did not really understand what she said. My mind told me she was a bit crazy. Yet she seemed to understand the language of my hair, and my hair seemed to be saying a lot about me. After two hours, the "new me" was ready. I looked into the mirror. My hair did not look happier yet. But I had made the decision to invite creativity back into my life.

After my visit to the hair stylist, I started to believe my inner voice, which had told me that I needed more creativity in my life. Some weeks later, I started a drawing class.

I still wanted to live abroad. I knew that I would regret it if I never realized my dream. When a friend of mine had left for Singapore a year earlier, I felt such a strong yearning that it hurt. At the time, Paolo had said that I had already packed my suitcases. Now I pushed Paolo to send some job applications to Sweden.

Four weeks later, we were together in the living room one evening after work. I couldn't wait to know the results of his applications, so I asked him while sitting on the sofa, "What is the status of your applications?" He was standing in the middle of the living room, and suddenly his complete body language changed. He became stiff, looked at me accusingly, and said, "And how will we organize a move when I get this job?"

I looked at him, puzzled. What was so difficult about organizing a move? So I said calmly, "Well, if you have a job there, we will move there, and then I will look for a job, too. I think the only question I need to answer is how to move the cats, whether I'll do it by car or by airplane."

Suddenly, he panted for air and his eyes grew big with horror. He said, "Move all this stuff? That will be chaos, complete chaos!" He raised his hands in the air with desperation. I looked at this large man and saw a little child in a panic. In that moment, I became aware that he would never move to another country. He had done it once, but he had been a child when he moved to Germany with his parents. Paolo was just too afraid to move again. It had taken me five years to understand this.

One month later, on a warm night in August, I decided that it was the right time to talk about our future. I was thirty-five years old. I wanted to plan when we would have children. Paolo sat next to me on the sofa. I looked at him and said, "Paolo, I have a question. When do you want to have children? You know that I just got a new job—a better job—with a different company. Now would be a good time to decide when we should have children."

Paolo did not even look at me. His eyes were glued to the TV. I looked at him expectantly. He had always said that he wanted to have children. I thought that he would tell me that he wanted to start now, preferably today. I had a smile on my face. He grunted and said, "I don't know."

I could not believe his words. Had he really said that he didn't know? I did not want to give up so easily and insisted, "Well, I am thirty-five years old, and I want to think through our life together. I want to know what career plans I should make, and I want to decide with you when it would be the best time to have children. Can't you just think about when it would be right for you?"

He looked at me and said in a harsh tone, "I have no idea. I don't know what I want in life. I have no idea when I want to have children."

I couldn't believe it. Was this really the man I loved? A man who had no idea about what he wanted in life? I sighed. Sometimes I asked myself whether there was anything that he knew about his life.

The months passed and we weren't able to create any mutual dreams to pursue. Paolo had long complained about the cats and their hair; these complaints increased and painful discussions became normal. One evening in January 2008, I was standing in our open kitchen and finishing with the dishes. Paolo sat on the sofa, the remote control of the PlayStation in his hands. He said, "It's always so dirty with the cat hair. You have to clean more." He did not even turn around to look at me. His eyes were on the game on the screen, darting here and there to follow the enemy. The TV made a *trr* sound. It seemed he had killed some virtual opponent.

I hated this sound. Sometimes I asked myself how much of the hero that he could have been in real life was wasted on his online avatar. Why didn't he just stop hiding in a virtual world and start living in the real world? I didn't know. "But why do I have to do everything myself?" I asked him. I felt desperate about this years-long discussion. Was I his cleaning lady with a task list so long that I could never finish it? Furthermore, it seemed that I never did the tasks correctly. I never was able to meet his expectations.

"That is your job. You have to do it," he said in a dismissive tone. I was sick and tired of our ongoing arguments. I did not know how to convince him of my needs and desires. I looked at his profile. How could I connect with this man who seemed so unreachable? He had grown so distant from me. Did I really know the man on the sofa? Where was the man I had fallen in love with? Was he still there? I did not know anymore. I felt powerless. His tone was the same tone that his father used to speak to his mother. I had never heard them say anything positive about each other. Instead, they just blamed each other for their own unhappiness. Paolo and I were on the same path. I did not want to continue on that path.

"You talk to me in the same way that your father talks to your mother," I said.

"No, I am not talking to you the way my father talks to my mother," he spit out. "You are crazy. You have to clean more. I can see cat hair everywhere and it is repulsive." A deep pain entered my heart. I looked at him. Was it possible that he had lost respect for me? I tried to calm down. The pressure in my heart grew stronger. Tears started to run down my face.

"Paolo, can we stop fighting for a moment, please? I can't go on like this. It's too much for me. Can't you just give me a hug?" I so desperately longed for a connection with him.

He turned his head and said with disgust in his voice, "No. I will not do it." I remembered that I had begged him once to promise that we would always reconcile after a conflict. We had never done this. I normally went to bed alone, and he would play his games in front of the TV. The next morning, we would get up and wait for the next fight. I did not want to continue this way anymore.

"Paolo, I can't continue like this. I can't. I want us to go to couples counseling." I had to say it. It was my last chance to solve the situation.

"I will never go to couples counseling with you," he said. His words hit me like a hammer. I had not expected this response.

"But you said so. Don't you remember? When Ina and Markus had their crisis?" His words had been my lifeline. I had trusted in them.

"I don't remember. And anyhow, all the problems we have are your problems."

In that moment, the pain in my heart became unbearable. An intense hurt hit my complete body with the force of a torrent of water rushing through a dry canyon after a heavy rain. The sensations became too much for me to handle. I left my body and felt that I could see it from above, an empty body like a dead shell made out of flesh and blood. How dead I was.

The feeling of nothing became unbearable, and I formed a fist with my right hand and hit my left arm. I had not done this for a long time. The intensity of the punches increased and the pain increased, but I felt a bit more alive. In the middle of the living room with Paolo, I was there all alone, only me and the pain and the dull sound of the punching. After some minutes, I started to feel that there was still life in my body. I looked at my left arm, which was now red. The bruises would appear soon, and for the next few days they would remind me that there was still some life in my body.

Paolo looked at me with abhorrence. Without moving from his seat, he said, "You are insane."

I looked at him. Even though I knew that it was too much to ask for, I just longed for his embrace and his acceptance of me and my way of coping with psychic suffering. Then he stopped talking to me, focusing on his game once more, and I went to bed alone.

My self-harming behavior wasn't a regular occurrence. At that point, I did it during situations of extreme stress in my relationship with Paolo, when I had completely abandoned myself and allowed him to violate my boundaries. Some time after this incident with Paolo, a therapist told me that I wouldn't be able to heal this behavior, that I would self-harm for my whole life. But since that time, I have learned to respect my limits and listen to my needs, and I haven't done it anymore.

Two weeks later, I went to my first Ashtanga Yoga class. The Yoga center was close to the Viktualienmarkt (victuals market) in the center of Munich, where all types of delicious tropical fruits were sold. I entered the hall through huge wooden doors. Indirect lighting in the floor made the walls seem to shimmer. Opposite me, sunlight shone softly through white curtains. In front of the window was a huge wooden boat with a Buddha statue in it. The hall was silent, with a hint of incense in the air. Three people were already sitting on their dark red mats. I went to the shelves on my right side and got a mat, looked for a spot in the very back, and sat down. Slowly, the hall filled up with people. Some of them greeted each other.

Suddenly, a blonde woman with bright eyes entered the room. She was accompanied by a special energy of joy and lightness. She seemed to be floating through the room like a fairy. She sat down in front of the group and smiled at each one of us. Then she said, "I am Nadine. I am your Ashtanga Yoga teacher." She paused and then continued: "For those of you who are new to Ashtanga, you have chosen the most strenuous form of Yoga." There was laughter in the room. I looked at her eyes and I felt her energy. I knew that one day I wanted to transmit the same energy that she did. I did not care how strenuous the Yoga was.

Even though my relationship was difficult, I continued to improve my life and realize my dreams. I silently accepted the fact that Paolo would never move abroad, and I decided to apply for a job with a Taiwanese company that required travel within Europe and sometimes a visit to the headquarters in Taiwan. In this way, I hoped to fulfill my hunger to live abroad, and I hoped to save my relationship.

I started the job and traveled to Taiwan in March 2008. One night, I sat with my two colleagues in a little bar at the shore of the Bin Tan Lake in Taipei in a simple and friendly room with wooden benches and tables and a ceramic floor. Through the windows, I could see how the lights of the suspension bridge that allowed pedestrians to cross to the other shore reflected in the shimmering water, which was an emerald-turquoise color during the day. We all had just started new jobs in the European office of the company and had stayed in Taipei for two weeks for training. During the day we were in the office building, listening to the different presentations of the products, and at night we went to the little bar to while away the evening hours. My colleagues, Steve and Ingo, enjoyed their beers, and I drank my fruit tea with fresh pineapple and mango. Steve was in his late forties, a British gentleman with a fine sense of humor. He had short blond hair and vivid blue eyes. He was vibrating with ideas and enthusiasm. Ingo was German, a couple of years younger than me, and had lived for several years in Dubai. We talked about the differences between cultures and what we had noticed during our training.

Steve commented, "Have you noticed that the younger people never speak if their manager is speaking?" I nodded. It seemed that there were strict rules about hierarchy and who was allowed to talk. I had noticed that my female Asian colleagues who had less work experience than I did looked at me with a special admiration. The Asian team was motivated, fully engaged, and dynamic. They had taken care of us with a special loving energy. Each morning, we were picked up. At lunch, we were invited to a restaurant, where they introduced us to their food. They also spent their evenings and weekends with us to show us Taipei and their culture. As independent as I was, I had never experienced so much care before, neither in private life nor on a business trip.

Suddenly, Steve changed the topic. He put down the professional mask, his voice became soft and loving, and his eyes had a special light as he said, "My ex-wife and I stayed together for the sake of our children until they were grown. Then we got divorced. Six months ago, I met the woman I love. The moment I saw her, I knew that she would be the love of my life. I want to spend the rest of my life with her. I miss her. I'll be so glad to see her when I return home." His tone was firm and definite. For a moment I thought, *How happy this woman must be with him!*

Then Ingo spoke about his love, his voice full of enthusiasm. He said, "I went to the Landshuter Hochzeit, a big medieval festival that takes place near Munich, with a friend. I saw her among all the visitors. When I saw her, I knew that she was the one. We started talking and we did not stop talking. At the time, we both were in relationships. We left those partners. I am so grateful to be with her. We want to get married soon." He was so full of appreciation for his partner. Their future seemed to be already written; they had a common dream. I looked at the happy faces of my two colleagues. I had nothing to say.

I had never managed to persuade Paolo to arrange a future with me. When I had asked him where he wanted to go on holiday in the summer, his answer was, "I do not know." When I had asked him a year earlier when he wanted to have children with me, his answer was, "I do not know." How often I had heard this sentence. Sometimes I felt that I was carrying a heavy bag on my back: Paolo. I was exhausted and sad because it seemed that he had no dreams at all and that there was no possibility of planning a future together. I felt sad because I had nothing to share with my colleagues. I remembered my continual fights with Paolo while I sat listening to my colleagues. They had so much love in their voices, so much appreciation. How did Paolo talk about me? No, Paolo would not have those emotions in his voice while talking about me. Did he appreciate anything about me? I did not know anymore. A soft voice in my head said, *But shouldn't it be this way? Shouldn't your partner talk this way about you?* Silently, I answered myself: *Yes, it should be this way.* Definitely, my relationship was far from being my dream of how it should be. How could I achieve this with Paolo if he blamed only me? I had to find a solution.

One week later, I flew to Munich, and Paolo picked me up at the airport. Due to my tiredness after the flight, I forgot to wish him Happy Birthday. He felt rejected and I felt guilty.

I went to a Yoga class with my sister one week later. After the class, we crossed the Viktualienmarkt, with its greenish wooden booths in the heart of Munich, where different delicacies, colorful fruits and vegetables, were sold during the day. My heart felt heavy. I knew that I had to make a decision that would change my life. We went downstairs to the Marienplatz train station. Waiting for the train in the underground station with reddish columns, I could not keep my secret. The burden was too great.

"Anna, I think I have to give away my cats to continue my relationship with Paolo," I said. She gave me a strange look. In that moment, I felt a horrible pain in my soul. I had spoken it aloud for the first time. I had to choose between my cats and my partner. I had never imagined that I would end up in this situation.

I remembered how we had picked them out together, two tiny little balls of wool. Was it fair to give them up? No. I would feel guilty for the rest of my life. I loved them. Why had we reached this point? I didn't know. Paolo had never given me an ultimatum, but I felt that there was only one solution: decide between Paolo and my cats. Why did he expect this from me? I did not know. Our family's cats, Charly and Chloe, and our family's dog, Mimic, had saved my life when I was a child. Orlando had saved my life when I was an adult. I knew that a part of my soul would die without cats. The train entered the station. I gave my sister a kiss and left her without a word. I was not yet ready to make a decision.

Four weeks later, I went to a trade show in Hannover. It was a bright, clear Sunday morning when I left the apartment to drive to work, where I would catch the bus that would take my colleagues and me to Hannover. The birds were singing outside. I took a final look at the apartment. It looked fine to me, even though I had not had time to clean the floors because I had needed to pack my belongings. I tried to calm myself by telling myself that Paolo wouldn't be angry. He knew that I had to leave on Sunday morning. Was there any rule that I always had to be the one to clean the apartment? I was not sure.

The next day, the trade show started. I stayed with my colleagues at the booth all day. At the end of the day, I left the hall with two of my colleagues. I received a phone call. It was Paolo.

"Hi! How are you?" I answered the phone. I was happy to hear from him.

"The apartment was a mess when I returned yesterday. You did not clean the cat hair," he said angrily. I did not reply. I did not want my colleagues to become aware of this discussion.

"And the mango that you left got moldy. You are so dirty!" he screamed into the receiver. My colleague gave me a strange glance.

This time, I had to respond. "I am sorry. But when I left, the mango was all right. I left it because I thought that you might like it," I said. I had left the mango for him so that he had something to eat when he came home. I felt hurt that he had called me dirty.

"You are lying. You are so dirty!" he said and hung up.

My colleague looked at me and asked, her brow knitted, "He screamed at you because of a rotten mango?" I looked at her. Silently, I replied, *Yes, he screamed at me because of a rotten mango. No, I do not want to be treated like this.*

That night, I couldn't sleep. I lay in my bed while tears ran down my face. The relationship was over. When I returned home, I would leave him. I had made my decision. I had decided for myself and my cats. The price to give them up was too great.

On Friday, we returned home on the bus right after the trade show. I knew that my life would never be the same after my return. I arrived at our house at 3:00 a.m. Its white walls shown brightly in the light of the moon. I left my car, my heart a stone in my chest. Slowly, I went up the stairs and entered the apartment. How many times had I entered this door? I could not remember. I stepped into the corridor with its Mediterranean paving tiles in warm and soft reddish-brown tones. At the other end, I saw the pale yellow open kitchen with the giant exhaust hood softly lit by the moonlight, which shone through the huge terrace door.

I glanced at the halfway open door in front of me, which led to the bedroom. There was no light on, so Paolo was asleep. It was a relief. I did not want to talk to him. When I had left this place six days earlier, I had never imagined that I would return and my life would change forever. The apartment was the same. Yet inside myself, everything had changed. I tiptoed into the kitchen and sat down on a chair in the dark, surrounded by the silhouettes of the furniture. It was the end of my dream of a relationship, the end of my dream of a common future and children. What had we done to reach this point? I sat there motionless, feeling darkness and pain and knowing that I had made the right decision.

Suddenly, Paolo emerged from the gloom of the bedroom, his steps slow. He asked in a sleepy voice, "What are you doing out here? Why don't you come to bed?"

For a moment, I again saw the man I had fallen in love with. I gulped down my tears and said, "Nothing. I'm coming." I went into the bedroom, got changed, and lay down next to him in the bed. My body was stiff and tense like a wooden doll, and I kept as close as I could to the edge on my side of the bed. I already knew the truth that Paolo was not yet aware of. This knowledge was a burden on my heart. I hoped daylight would arrive soon.

In the morning, I got up first and made coffee alone. Outside, the sun was shining brightly. My heart and my stomach felt heavy. Paolo woke up and came into the kitchen. I couldn't wait any longer. So I said what I had to say, briefly and directly: "Paolo, I have to talk to you. Our relationship is over. I am leaving you." He wasn't surprised. We started talking about our broken dreams. For a moment, we recovered our old love while sharing the precious memories of our time together: how I had eaten peaches all day long during our holiday in Bordeaux, those crazy first nights in his old apartment, my faux pas when I had called him an idiot. We couldn't figure out how we had arrived at the point we were at; we just knew that it was over. A relationship is not only habit. It needs a deep connection and common dreams. Ours did not have the connection or the dreams. A relationship needs to change and to evolve over time. Ours hadn't.

Later that day, I went outside on the balcony, leaning against the bucket for the plants, feeling the warmth of the sun on my skin. It was already afternoon and I was still in my pajamas.

Paolo came out and said, "If you had not made this decision, I would have done it within a few months. I was about to lose my respect for you." My inner voice told me that his respect had left long ago; he just had not been aware of it. Even though it hurt me, I appreciated his honesty. Finally, he was communicating his feelings. I just listened to his words; there was no need to say anything. It did not matter anymore. He said, "You know, I always hoped that you'd change your mind, that you'd stop working and stay at home with our children." He had never mentioned this before. I had always told him that I would want to keep working if we had children. I would not compromise on this.

He continued, "Each time I was ill, my parents told me that it was the fault of the cats and that we should get rid of them." I was surprised. He had never told me this. His parents had never said anything to me. Paolo had told me at the beginning of our relationship that the cats in Italy all lived outside the house. How much did these comments influence Paolo? What else had his parents said to him about me? I remembered the look of reproach his mother had given me when I told her that I did not have any contact with my father. No contact with your family? That was unbelievable to an Italian woman.

Paolo said, "You never gave me a clear sign that it was too much for you. I never knew that you were suffering in our relationship." I thought about how many times I had stood in the kitchen crying, how many times I had begged him to stop yelling, how many times I had hurt myself because the fights went on and on. How much clearer could I have been?

Then he continued, "I always had the feeling that you never really trusted me. You know, when we were dancing and I tried to bend you back, you would never do it." Another subject we never had talked about openly. I knew that trust was my weak point, because I still didn't understand completely what it meant. I did not know that he had noticed. If he had told me earlier, I would have started therapy. Maybe we would have separated earlier, or maybe we would have found ways to deal with these issues. Now it was too late.

Finally, he said, "I also think you should forget about the sexual abuse, just forget about it." He wanted me to be normal and to forget about it. Forget about it? Forget about knowing inside myself that people who have suffered abuse in their childhood might do the same as adults? How could I ever forget this knowledge? How could I ever forget the shadow of my father? I couldn't understand why he wanted me to forget. But although I could not forget this subject, I knew that I had to come to terms with it. I wanted to look at it with peace. If I could look at it with peace, my partner would look at it with peace. How could I achieve this? I did not know yet.

Paolo went back into the apartment while I stayed on the terrace alone. Another failed relationship, another time that my partner had not respected me, and another time that I had the feeling it was all my fault. Could a relationship fail because of the fault of only one partner? Usually, it is both of them who fail. Yet it was my second relationship to fail. I had missed something that I should have learned earlier. I still wasn't able to trust completely. And I could not solve my problem alone. I had to ask for help. I decided to start therapy.

My relationship with Paolo had begun with hope and true feelings. But we got caught in a vicious cycle of withdrawal and rejection. There was a lack of honesty and a lack of trust in each other and in our relationship. We repeated what we had learned from our parents because we had not yet healed our childhood wounds. I also believe that our relationship didn't work out because we were just too different. I loved cats and he didn't. I needed change and he hated it. I wanted to live abroad and he didn't. I was active and engaged in sports and he wasn't. I wanted to combine work and family and he didn't. Our approaches to life were just too different.

After I broke up with Paolo, I felt liberated. Because it was my apartment, we agreed that he would move out. As an interim solution, I moved into the guest room while he stayed in the bedroom.

The next weekend, Paolo went to Mannheim to see his friends and family. When he returned, suddenly everything had changed. He told me daily that I was unfair to him and that I was the person who was solely responsible for the separation. He told me that I hadn't given him clear enough signs that our relationship was bad. Each morning when he emerged from the bedroom, he looked at me with tears in his eyes. I could understand his pain, yet I didn't feel able to help him because I seemed to cause his pain. One time, after I told him again that I didn't see a future for us, he withdrew into the bathroom and I heard his loud sobbing. Desperate, I phoned one of his friends in Mannheim and asked him to talk to Paolo, because I was worried about him.

I felt horrible while we still lived together. Sometimes, I arrived at work in tears because I did not know how to handle the situation. If it were not my own apartment, I would have moved out at once. I felt stuck and I didn't understand why he had made a 180 degree turn regarding our separation. We ended up in a psychologist's office, where I reaffirmed that I did not want to continue our relationship. Finally, he accepted my decision, and after three months he moved out.

One night while we still lived together, my inner child brought up again the most painful question that I had ever asked my parents. It was a dark night, just two weeks after our separation. Paolo was already in the bedroom, and I was in the guest room, unable to find sleep. I had hoped to become normal in my relationship with Paolo. I had failed. My mother had always said, "You are intelligent." When I had left Michael, my late grandfather's partner had told me, "Don't worry, you are intelligent." Was life all about rationality? Intelligence was all well and good, but what I longed for was a deep connection with my partner. What would my success in business be worth if I were isolated and alone and had nobody to share my life with? *The sexual abuse must have destroyed my ability to connect lovingly with a man,* I thought. This well-known deep pain, which had accompanied me for so many years, invaded my body one more time. It was a black hole below my feet that seemed to eat away at me, bit by bit. My heart felt as though it were being torn into pieces. The walls of my room became the dirt walls of my grave.

I couldn't bear to stay in the house any longer. I went out

into the garage, started up my red Mini Cooper, and drove out into the night. The sky was dark, clear, and full of stars. The entrance to the highway was just two minutes away. It was nearly midnight and the highway was empty. I thought, *It's better so.* Nobody else would be on the road. I hadn't done it for many years, and that day I had to do it again. I leaned on the gas pedal. The speedometer went up: 105 miles per hour, 120 miles per hour, 125 miles per hour. I pushed my foot even harder against the gas pedal. The guard railing at the left side was my guide. Trees and bushes became silhouettes of volatile illusions. The car lost its stability, the steering wheel moved on its own between my hands, my speed was at its limit. My mask shattered. My complete body was shaking. And my soul was screaming. Tears ran down my face like a flood breaking down a dam. I was sobbing. The street became indefinite. *What do I want: To live? Or to die?* I couldn't answer. The pain was too great for me. I became the little girl that I once had been and cried to my parents in the darkness of the night, "Why have you done this to me? Why have you done this to me? Why have you given me life, only to take it away from me?"

The question tortured me. After twenty minutes, my tears began to dry and my foot decided to soften its pressure on the gas pedal. The car slowed down. I left the highway and turned around. I would continue living. When I returned, I drove to the little lake that was some minutes away from my apartment. The gentle hill with bushes was a haunting silhouette in the night. I left the car, walked down the short path, and lay down on the grass, near the shore. I felt the cold stones of the rocks in the grass against my back. The sky was clear and full of stars. The moon left a shimmering glance on the lake. I felt the chilly night air on my skin. I was exhausted but I had survived.

Victims can become perpetrators. I had read that in a book about sexual abuse some years earlier. I had never told it to Paolo. For a while that evening, the burden and the guilt about my possible shadow had been too much for me. And it was my responsibility to deal with it and its effects. It was my responsibility to make the best of it. I wanted to have a positive relationship, and I wanted to be a good mother. I had no idea how to do this; I only knew that I had to do it. The darkness of the night surrounded me with a comforting cloak. I looked up at the sky and silently asked for help. I was on a road of no return.

That was the last time that I went out on the highway to test my life. As I continued with my healing process, the deep wound in my heart mended and the question of why my parents had done what they did to me became insignificant because I had found a deeper meaning in life.

Despite my sorrow about my failed relationship, I continued to make plans for my future. Two weeks after that night, I met my sister in Schwabing. Spring was in the air. The weather was warm and the energy was vibrant. The first fresh green leaves had appeared on the trees. We went to the English Garden, where we found a shady spot in the grass in a clearing surrounded by beeches and majestic weeping willows. We could hear and see the rippling of the little creek that crossed the English Garden. The air was full of the scent of fresh grass and flowers. We unpacked our delicious cakes, which we had just bought in one of the cafés on Leopoldstrasse. While having our picnic, I said, "I've thought about where I want to live. It's not Italy because I don't fit in well with the culture. The role of a woman is too traditional there. I want to go to Spain. I've never been there but it feels like the right place for me to live." For a long time, I had dreamed about living abroad. Now, as a single person, I wanted to realize my dream. I had to do it. I continued to explain my plans to my sister: "In August, I want to go to Barcelona to see whether I like the city and to start learning Spanish."

She nodded. She knew about my dream and replied, "Maybe one day we can live together abroad." I smiled.

I had wanted to live abroad since I was a child. Maybe I was motivated by the fact that my grandfather was Croatian, and even though my mother was German, I never felt completely German. Spain was also far away from my father and the continuous threat that he might show up at my door. For many years, I had forced myself to stay, first to please my grandfather and later because of Paolo. Now I would follow my inner voice and do what felt right for me.

Swimming in the Vortex of Change

Some months later, I went on a date with an English work colleague, Sam. He was attractive, with dark brown eyes, and I sometimes caught him staring at me. As with Paolo, I couldn't manage to kiss him at the end of our date. I ran away and felt deeply ashamed and desperate.

The next Monday, I sat on an airplane at Munich Airport next to Andy, a Taiwanese colleague, whom I had met the first time the preceding March in Taipei. He was a pleasant and deeply respectful man. He had just told me that he wanted to buy cutlery from WMF for his wife when we returned the following Friday. His wife loved WMF, a German tableware manufacturer with a long history. I was so distracted that I could hardly focus on his words.

While we fastened our seat belts, Andy asked me, "And you? How are things going?" I looked at him. What should I tell him? I felt trapped in a fine black spiderweb, which seemed to accompany me my whole life; with every move I made, it became tighter. I had left the first man I wanted to spend my life with. I had fallen in love with another man, and I had run away again. Thoughts ricocheted inside my head. I could find no tranquility within. Why did I see love as a threat? It should be a beautiful experience. I took a breath. I knew it was my past that produced my fear, a fear so deep that I felt as though I were dying. When would my past stop haunting me?

I wondered what I was supposed to tell him, and while fighting back my tears, I said calmly and professionally, "Well, my relationship did not work out and we broke up." Andy looked at me with his warm brown eyes and said, "I'm sure that you'll find the right man." My ears were able to hear his words, and somehow their softening energy got through to my heart.

Andy's words helped me believe in myself. This was just one time—and there were many times—when I became aware of the gap between my negative self-perception, one that was full of self-doubt and self-criticism, and how other people perceived me. The comments of others gave me confidence and helped me to believe in myself, step by step. As a survivor of childhood trauma, I tended (and sometimes still tend) to focus on the trauma. I wasn't able to see my own inner resources. My psychic scales were out of balance. The trauma on the one side was a heavy weight; I had nothing to put on the side of the resources because I didn't see them. The observations of my friends helped me to put something on the resources side of the scale, and thus my emotional scales became more balanced.

Sam contacted me two weeks after our first date and the kissing disaster. We went out again, and I used the same procedure that I had used with Paolo because I still didn't know any better: I pushed away my fears, kissed him, and had sex with him. For me, it was the beginning of a relationship. I saw him at work every once in a while, but we were never able to meet regularly due to his business trips. I didn't mind because after my recent separation from Paolo, I was reorganizing my life and eager to see my friends and start new hobbies.

Four weeks later, we sat in his car on our way to a spa. I lightly touched his right hand, which lay on the gearshift. He turned his head to look at me, and we smiled at each other. Green meadows with grazing cows and the foothills of the Alps passed us by as though we were in a movie. The mountains started as a green slope, which transformed itself into a dark wood, and ended up as sharp gray points of stone, which were partly hidden by dark gray clouds.

Later in the spa, we went to the outdoor hot tub. Sam leaned against a wall in the tub and closed his eyes. He looked relaxed and seemed to enjoy the warm underwater current. Just then a mother with her baby swam close to him. As he opened his eyes and saw them, his face softened and a smile appeared on his face. He gestured to me to look at the child. I looked at the mother and her child and then at him again. I had never seen him with such brilliant eyes before; at work, his eyes were dark, cold, and practically lifeless. I had never thought that he liked children so much. I imagined him as the father of our children and started to smile myself.

The next day, I flew to Barcelona to learn Spanish. During the two weeks that I was gone, he did not text me or phone me. I didn't worry because I knew that he was a loner. When I returned, he went on holiday and then on business trips, so we rarely saw each other. Sometimes I struggled with this, but in general, I didn't worry too much about it, because the few times we did get together were the most wonderful times I had ever had with a man. His travels became just a part of our relationship.

In November, we flew to Taipei together on a business trip, and I spent most of the flight with my head on his shoulder. We arrived Sunday night in Taipei and stayed at the same hotel near the Bin Tan Lake where I had stayed almost a year earlier.

Sam cautiously snuck out of his hotel room each night and came to my room. In the morning, he returned to his hotel room. I had never spent so many nights in a row with him.

Our relationship was a secret at work because, as Sam had explained to me, he kept his private life and his professional life strictly separate. I accepted this because I wanted to give us the time we needed to find out whether we really fit together.

On Thursday, my colleagues and I gathered in the huge, windowless assembly room. The artificial light made all the faces look a little green. The different business units from the five continents were to present their planning for the following year. About three hundred Taiwanese colleagues sat in rows, just like in a theater, to listen to us. Now they looked at Sam, who stood in the front of the room, professional and convincing as always, explaining our planning for the next twelve months while making his jokes.

Then it was my turn. In the moment when he turned the podium over to me, he looked into my eyes, and I could see a love and softness in them that I had never seen before. I was in heaven.

That night, we drove to dinner with three other colleagues as our manager made one of his jokes: "Sam, now we will look for a woman for you. You have been single too long. You need a wife." Sam smiled. Everybody in the car was laughing. Sam was famous for being a bachelor. He answered, "I have not yet found the right woman." I just sat there silently and tried to tell myself that he did not mean it the way it sounded. Our secret hurt; I would have preferred honesty.

Friday night, we strolled across the bridge over the Bin Tan Lake. The street was busy with people returning from work. Different restaurants offered freshly cooked local delicacies, such as Stinky Tofu on the Road. We smelled the various foods and ordered several delicious-smelling dishes of tofu and vegetables to go. Then we went to the water's edge, sat down on one of the steps, and ate.

My shoulder leaned against Sam's shoulder, and I could feel the warmth of his body. The lake was now full of little boats where lovers enjoyed the peacefulness of the night under a sky full of stars. On the other side of the shore, there was the bar where my colleagues had opened my eyes about my relationship with Paolo. Now I sat here with Sam. I loved him and I wanted a future with him. Once, he had said he wasn't sure where he wanted to live in the future, and I had told him that I would go anywhere in the world with him. I knew I could do so. When I love a man, everything becomes possible.

On Saturday, our paths separated at Taiwan Taoyuan International Airport, in the coolness and cleanliness of the huge white departure hall. During the week, we had been together twenty-four hours a day. Every moment with him had been special and warm for me. I had never felt such warmth before. It was a luxury, because at home I saw him only once every two to three weeks due to his extensive travels. He gave me a clandestine hug behind a wall so that our colleagues wouldn't see us.

When I arrived in Singapore, I sent him a text message. He never answered. He had disappeared again. He wouldn't be available by phone or by Skype or by email.

One day later, I got ill. I knew that it was a message from my body that the situation was too much for me. Filled with medication, I sat on a plane. Next to me was a woman from Australia who was going home to Poland to visit her family. When I got on the plane in Singapore, she had already been traveling for six hours. We started to talk about our lives.

"I have a relationship with a very nice man," I told her. "We met five months ago." I heard the doubt in my voice. "I hope to have a future with him. I'd love to live with him."

When we left the airplane in Munich, she said, "I wish you luck with your relationship." I looked at her. I couldn't tell her how much I wanted this relationship, maybe partly as a sign that I had overcome my father's influence in my life. But my inner voice told me to be cautious.

Our relationship continued. We would have some wonderful moments, and then he would disappear. Slowly, I formed the impression that he was a shadow that always moved some steps behind me. I could turn and twist but would never be able to get hold of him. When I would say this to him, he would always say, "Natalie, you are too fast. I am like a turtle and slow moving."

It was true: I was fast when I knew what I wanted. I hoped that one day we would move at the same pace.

Two months later, I finally had my first session with a therapist. I climbed up the stairs of an old office building close to Marienplatz. The wooden planks creaked with each step. I counted the steps to calm myself: "Eighteen, nineteen, twenty." Then I stood in front of a small wooden door. I pressed the bell and waited. The creaking sound on the other side of the door indicated that somebody was coming to the door. It opened. An elderly woman with short red hair faced me. I said, "I have an appointment with Dr. Mueller, the psychologist." She nodded and indicated that I should take a seat on one of the wooden chairs that stood in the corridor. I sat down. The hallway was long and narrow. To my left was a window with some red flowers on the sill. What should I expect now? I did not know. I knew that I wanted to overcome the negative patterns begun in my past, so that I could have a healthy relationship.

What would the therapist be like? How would I connect with her? I was nervous. I had little idea what therapy was all about. I had asked for a female psychologist. I still felt fear if I was alone with a man, whether at work or with a doctor. This fear had accompanied me all my life. I knew that it was from my childhood and had nothing to do with the man I was with.

A door opened and a small woman with long gray hair that hung a little untidily to her shoulders, an ankle-length gray wool skirt, and a brown wool turtleneck walked down the hallway. "Ms. Jovanic?" I nodded and stood up to follow her. Her office was small. On the right side stood a table with her computer, and next to that was the sofa. Near the door was a shelf full of books. On the left side stood a chair with a little table, and another chair with pink cushions was in front of it. She gestured to me to sit down there. She sat opposite me. I was wondering what I should tell her. I had no idea what was important. I looked at her and hoped instantly that she'd ask me some questions. I did not know how to talk about my inner world. She looked at me. After some moments, I gave up on my wish for a question and hoped that I would say the right things, the things that would be important to my healing.

I began my story. "When I was three years old, I was sexually abused. My father and my stepfather were both manipulative. My mother died of cancer when I was nineteen, and my father keeps sending me unwanted letters. I have just left my boyfriend, and he blames me for the breakup. I want to solve this problem."

She looked at me with a grimace full of pity and sadness and said, "You are telling me such horrible things and you are smiling." I knew that I was smiling. What else did she want me to do? It was the only story I had. I did not have any better experience to share. How I would have loved to share a story full of lightness and joy. But I couldn't. I felt worse than ever. Her words and her pity made me shrink back in my seat. *That's it? Nothing that I can do? I'll be stigmatized my whole life?* Looking at her did not give me any hope. I left her office, more desperate and disoriented than ever.

The months passed. Between my work, Yoga, therapy, and Sam, my schedule was full. On a sunny day in April, I had lunch with Sam on a workday. We had a lot of fun together. Sam could make me really laugh if he wanted to. On our return to our office building, a colleague saw us together. The moment he saw us, the expression on his face changed. An hour later, he came to my desk and said with a big smile on his face, "Tell me the name of your boyfriend! I know that you have a new boyfriend. A woman who looks so beautiful and has such a wonderful smile has a new boyfriend."

I looked at him. I knew that he had seen Sam and me together. How much I would have liked to tell him, "Sure, I have a new boyfriend. You know it. Look at the man who sits at the desk next to mine at work." But I knew that I had to lie. Sam would never tolerate this. So I said, "No, I do not have a partner." I had been lying now for more than nine months. Patience can be hurtful.

The next day, Sam went on a business trip again, and while he was away, I went out for dinner with my colleagues. It was just before Easter. We sat in a small restaurant with dark wooden tables and seats. We had a table occupying the right corner, and I was jammed onto a huge corner bench, right in the middle between two colleagues to my right and two to my left. We were an international crowd: Germans, English, Taiwanese, Malaysians, and Serbians. The only one missing was Sam, who had flown home that day to visit his parents for a two-week holiday. I missed him and was engrossed in my thoughts about him.

Suddenly, a colleague said, "Well, what is our grumpy Sam doing right now? I booked him a flight to Dublin." And another one said in her flirty, upbeat voice, "I assume he is going back to his girlfriend. He was in love with a woman from Dublin just before he came to Munich two years ago. Anyway, he has a girl in every port." I looked at her, deeply shocked. Her words were a dagger in my heart. Could this be? Everybody at the table laughed and agreed with her: Sam had a girl in every port.

I was stunned and silent. Why hadn't Sam told me that he'd be visiting his ex? I had never asked him what he did when he was away. I had just trusted him. Now I sat in the middle of my colleagues while a thunderstorm raged in my heart. The part of me that fought for freedom said, *That idiot! I will not allow him to hurt me anymore*, and left the relationship that very moment. The other part, sweet and soft like a flower, said, *I know they are wrong. People can talk all they want, but I know how different he is when he's alone with me. I love him. I don't want to lose him.* The freedom fighter responded, *You're just afraid of being abandoned. But I don't need anybody. I will not allow anybody to hurt me!* The freedom fighter was powerful and fierce. I wanted to cry. I wanted desperately to be alone in my pain, and I was in the middle of people smiling and laughing about their Casanova colleague in the moment of my saddest defeat. I put on my child-hood mask and kept smiling through my despair.

Holding my mobile phone under the table, I texted Sam: "What the hell are you doing in Dublin? Why didn't you tell me? Why are you so mean to me?" I couldn't contain my anger. I got an acknowledgment of receipt. It had arrived. As usual, I received no answer. This time, I could not bear it. I had to communicate with him or I would burst.

I texted him again: "I need an answer. You are a coward. Tell me, why do you treat me so badly? Why didn't you tell me?!" No answer.

Like a robot, I stayed in the group and swallowed my tears. *Just don't let them see your pain.* The dinner seemed to never end, but finally we paid and left the restaurant. When I was on the street, I had air to breathe again. I lit a cigarette to ease my pain. I had begun to smoke a few months earlier to deal with my inner stress. Before the dinner, I had promised to give a ride to a colleague. I had to keep my word. On our way to my car, I burst into tears. I couldn't hold them back anymore; the pain in my heart was too great. I told her about my relationship with Sam.

She looked at me and said, "You have a relationship with Sam? I didn't know!" Of course, she hadn't. It had been a secret. I had always hated that it was a secret. It had felt wrong. I drove to her apartment, and she invited me upstairs to talk. I tried to phone Sam. He had turned off his phone. I stood in my colleague's apartment with my confusion about what was going on between us.

Four days later, I sat in the psychologist's office and said, "Well, for me, it is over now. I have already packed up the stuff he had in my apartment and sent it back to him."

Dr. Mueller looked at me with cool eyes and said, "You are complicated. You will always find complicated men."

I looked at her. Her words broke my heart. I knew that my past had been difficult, but did that mean that I would find only partners like Sam or Paolo? That was all I would get in a relationship? I could not believe it. I wanted to have a loving and respectful relationship. What was so complicated about that? I looked at her, a woman in her forties, whom I sometimes saw as a gray mouse, yet she was the psychologist, she was the authority. If she said it, it must be true. The accuracy of her words hit me deep in my heart, and I decided to learn.

I looked at her and asked, "So what would be the right thing to do?" And she told me that it was not yet finished and that I had to talk to him. I did not really understand what she meant. Her words made no sense to me, but I decided to do what she said because I wanted to change.

Three weeks later, Sam came to my apartment late in the evening. It was a chilly night in May. When he entered, he gave me a hug. His eyes had lost life. He was cool and distant. I explained to him that his behavior had hurt me and that I wanted to have a future with him. His body went rigid; it seemed as though his loving and human part had left his body and he was now a robot. I knew this change. He was a mirror of me. He feared relationships, as I once had. But during the past few months, I had overcome much of my fear. He said coldly, "Sorry. I did not see any future. Not yet." His words hurt. I knew that I had to let him go. Yet his sudden change of behavior made it impossible to do so. An elastic strap seemed to encircle the two of us. The child within me wanted to save him, just as she had always wanted to save my father from loneliness and pain and lifelessness. So her little voice said, *You are strong, Natalie. You can be there for him. You cannot leave him alone like this. You have to save him.* Despite the clearness of the other parts of my psyche, I was not able to let him go.

We continued our relationship. It had a painful dynamic of closeness and rejection, and during the next months I was regularly ill and lost energy.

I couldn't end my relationship with Sam right away due to several reasons. I felt guilty because Paolo had told me that I hadn't given him enough time, and so I wanted to be sure to give Sam enough time. It was also easier for me to concentrate on saving him and healing his wounds instead of facing my own wounds. I believed that I could save him. I lacked a proper idea about the relationship I wanted and needed. In addition to this, I couldn't avoid seeing him because we saw each other at the office. It was like a mousetrap.

I did my best to manage the situation. I bought a book written for the person whose partner had a fear of commitment. As the book recommended, I focused on my own life. I started salsa dancing, and I also continued my own healing by contacting a facilitator for family constellation therapy.

A few days later, I rang the bell of the door of a two-story house in Munich. The building was in a quiet and peaceful neighborhood with green gardens and huge trees, close to a BMW factory. Birds were singing in the air. The door opened and I went upstairs to the second floor. Renate, the facilitator, stood in the doorway. She had white hair and soft blue eyes. Five years after reading about constellation therapy for the first time, I was now ready to give it a try. I wanted to heal my soul. I did not dare talk about my family in front of a group of strangers, so I preferred an individual session to a group session.

I explained my situation and the facts about my family to Renate. She looked at me and said, "You have a distant father, so you find distant men." I nodded. I was aware of the fact that my father influenced my selection of men: they were either unreachable and didn't love me or they wanted to change or possess me. Sometimes, they were all of these things. None of them had a capacity for intimacy. I wanted to get out of this dynamic. We made a constellation of my parents with stones. She told me that as a child, I hadn't been in the right place. I had taken over the responsibility of my parents. We had to put this in the right order. She told me that when I thought about my parents, I should tell myself one thing: *I was the child; you were the adults.* My body relaxed. The sentence touched me deeply. All my life, I had felt responsible for my mother's life and my father's life. Later, I had felt responsible for my partner's happiness and well-being. I started to repeat this sentence each night on my terrace.

My relationship with Sam continued. We saw each other every second or third week. Then he would leave on a business trip. He never phoned me and usually didn't answer when I phoned him. When he was in Munich, we went to the movies and took long walks at night. We would have dinner in our favorite Indian restaurant or we might have a long brunch on Sunday morning. Then we would spend the day in Murnau, close to the skiing area of Garmisch-Partenkirchen in the Alps.

In the mountains, we visited an exhibit of Der Blaue Reiter (The Blue Rider), a group of artists from almost one hundred years ago, including Vasily Kandinsky and Gabriele Münter. Murnau was a magical place in the Alps, full of nature and calmness. When Sam and I visited the exhibit, we had a lot of fun; he made humorous comments about the paintings and we reflected together on their meanings. Then we drove to the Starnberger See, a nearby lake, and spent the afternoon lying on the shore, enjoying the sun while we embraced each other.

On our way back, we took the curvy road through the Wuerm-tal, a wild and mystical valley with huge green trees, formed by the Wuerm River. I had traveled this road often in my child-hood. It led to the place where I had lived with my mother. I wanted to visit her grave. I parked the car at the cemetery. Sam waited outside. I entered the cemetery, and behind the little fountain with goldfish that was nearly green from the moss that grew on it, there was the old hall where my mother's funeral had taken place. Would my mother have died happier and more content if she'd had at least one satisfying relationship with a man? At the end of her life, I had the feeling that she struggled so much with her death because she had never been truly loved by a man, maybe not even by her father. I did not want to repeat her destiny. I wanted to give and receive true love. I turned left to the main road with huge, old trees and colorful graves full of flowers and old greenish gravestones. I arrived at the graves of my family, with the urns of my grandmother, my grandfather, and my mother.

I stood at their graves and connected in my mind's eye with my mother. I told her, "Dear Mami, I was the child; you were the adult. I honor how you have borne your destiny. I love you. Although I will leave Munich, you'll always be in my heart." I just stood there and felt the energy of my words. I knew that I'd never come back again. When I went to Barcelona, I would light a candle for her so that she would remain in my life.

When I returned to the car, Sam did not say a word. He just hugged me and moved me into the last spot of sunlight, so that I'd receive its warmth. I was deeply moved by his kind gesture. As we stood there, I knew that I had never felt so close to a man.

Despite all the childhood patterns that I relived with Sam, I also experienced for the first time in my life a sense of tenderness and caring from a man. The times we spent together were gentle, respectful, and loving. I was grateful for his company. He behaved like a gentleman and took care of me. We had fun together. We liked the same activities. I felt liked for the way I was, and I experienced a new lightness and tenderness with him. The week after our trip, he broke up with me. After this, I connected more deeply with my friends, and I started to share the truth about my childhood, including the sexual abuse. A few weeks later he returned, and I decided to give our relationship one last try.

After some weeks, I was in Dr. Mueller's office, and she suggested a visualization. I lay down on her sofa and went inside myself. I saw a galloping horse and a snail. The galloping horse was fast and strong and ran through life alone at high speed. The snail had a colorful house. It moved along *very* slowly—but steadily. It was vividly colored, full of curiosity, and had an immense capacity for love. This part loved and survived each crisis with Sam. It knew that love is the most important thing in life.

My therapist asked, "So what would happen if the horse and the snail met one day?" I saw a picture of a snail walking happily through the world at its slow pace and the horse at its back as its companion, attentive to the snail, being at its service.

Walking back to my car, I realized that the snail was my soul. For so many years, I had been convinced that the abuse had killed my soul and destroyed my capacity to love. Yet my soul had survived, hidden in its house, and it was now on its way to recovery. In the middle of deep inner chaos and desperate love-sickness, I had found my soul, a precious present.

Meanwhile, I started to have increasing problems with my manager at work. I tried to meet his expectations but failed. After a session with my therapist, in which I became aware that I would never meet his expectations, I quit my job and decided to move to Spain as soon as possible.

Summer passed. In October, I went to the wedding of a friend. At this stage, my third attempt with Sam had lasted three months. Alexandra was a former colleague and friend, and she had moved to Affoltern am Albis in Switzerland, close to Zurich, two years earlier. In the preceding year, I had visited her and her fiancé several times for a weekend. We had spent the time chatting about our lives, enjoying good food, and walking in the nearby hills.

The wedding took place in the city hall. Later, we all waited outside to celebrate the newly wedded couple. The October sun shone gently on my skin, and we were surrounded by green hills. Alexandra came outside with her bride's bouquet in her hands, and I remembered the many times I had hidden at weddings to make sure that I would not catch it, because I dreaded compromise with a man. This time, I just stood there and felt that I would love to receive it. Moments later, I held the elegant yellow bouquet of sunflowers in my hands, and I was proud that I had it. At thirty-six, I had overcome much of my fear of commitment.

Three days later, I spent a wonderful Sunday with Sam. On Monday, I received a panicked text from him: "I don't see a future with you. I feel horrible here, far away from home. I need to concentrate on my life." I wasn't really sure what he meant. But I knew that he was deeply unhappy in Munich, and I became worried for him. Then I became angry with him. I cared for him. I phoned a colleague, who now knew the truth, to tell him to kick his ass. Finally, I accepted the truth. We had broken up for the third time. I knew that it was over. My energy was gone.

I sat down on my balcony in the sun and had a cigarette. During our time together, I had lived my life and he had lived his life. I had overcome fears and started therapy. He had never done any work on himself. I had wanted to create a life together. I had seen our relationship as a tender plant that needed to be nurtured by both sides to grow and blossom out each day a bit more. He had never nurtured that plant. It would never work out if only I tended to the plant that was our relationship. It was time to let him go; there was no need to fight anymore. I had to focus on my own life. I was the most important person in my life.

The next day, I flew to Barcelona for a job interview—and I landed the position.

Even though the relationship with Sam was difficult, I had learned about my own process of how I commit to a relationship. I require both closeness and distance, so that I have the freedom to decide whether I really want to continue with a man. For the first time, I had had both feet in a relationship. It had been a painful experience, yet it had also been the relationship in which I had learned the most about myself.

I had to move to Barcelona within six weeks, so I got very busy preparing everything. One night in November 2009, someone rang my doorbell at 6:00 p.m. It was already dark outside. As always, I got up and pushed the button that would open the door. *It must be a delivery service,* I thought. I felt safe. I opened the door to my apartment, which was on the second floor, just under the roof, and waited in the doorway for the delivery. I heard a creeping sound of shoes in the darkness, as though somebody was going from door to door. He would not be lucky: the names were not written on the doors. Funny. Why didn't he turn on the light? *Poor guy, maybe he can't find the light.* I switched on the light.

Suddenly, my inner voice told me, *Go back into the apartment and close the door.* As quietly as a cat, I returned to my apartment and closed the door. I looked out the peephole. Who would be coming up the stairs? I had a premonition. I knew that it was him. My mind told me that it was not possible. *You have a secret address.*

I pressed my eye more cautiously against the peephole. I heard the ponderous footsteps come up the stairs. A doorbell rang on the first floor.

"Where does Jovanic live?" a male voice asked. My heart stood still. My body turned to ice. It was him. It was my father. He had found me. How could that be possible?

"You just have to go upstairs. It is the door on the right side," the friendly voice of my neighbor said. I had never told her not to tell anyone where I lived. I had wanted to be normal, just like everybody else. Who on Earth needs a secret address to get rid of her father? The steps came faster now and rushed up the final staircase. I saw a dark coat flying around the corner. A large, tall man approached my door. I saw his face. It was him; it was my father. Suddenly, all my security and protection went away.

I was transformed into the little child and then into the mouse in front of a mighty snake. I could hardly breathe. My arms and my legs turned to jelly.

Get away from the door. Hide in a secure place. My inner orders came directly. *Are there any secure places?* I wasn't sure. What if he managed to enter? I wouldn't be able to cope with that. I ran into the living room and grabbed my laptop, my mobile phone, and the telephone. While I ran into my bedroom, which was the room farthest away from the front door, I permitted myself a short glance at the door. The doorbell rang. I could see how the black shadow I had hidden from all my life showed itself against the white entrance door and also entered under the door. I would not allow it to get me. In the bedroom, I closed the door. What if he could open the door? I did not dare to finish this thought. Whom should I call first? Paolo. His new apartment was just five minutes away. I grabbed the mobile and hit the speed dial. My hands were shaking. I did not call the police due to my previous bad experience with them; when Wolfgang had beaten my sister, they had done nothing.

"Yes?" Paolo's voice answered.

"My father. My father has found me. He is at my apartment door," I said, crying like a baby. I had always told him that I would move to another apartment if my father found me. Now my father had found me, just two weeks before my planned move to Barcelona.

"My God. I am in Mannheim. I can't help you," he answered with preoccupation in his voice. Shit. I was alone. I knew when I left him that I would lose my protection. It was much easier to live with a partner than to live alone. I did not know what to say. The doorbell rang another time. While he tried to calm me, I contacted my dance partner, Tim, via Skype. I felt desperate. I did not care anymore whether my friends would judge me for having the father I had. I needed help. I needed protection. He was bigger than me. I needed him to go away. I would never, ever allow him to touch me again.

"Who else can you call?" Paolo asked me. A million ants seemed to be running up my arms and legs. My breathing was flat. I looked at the screen of my laptop. Tim had not yet replied. I heard how my father was knocking at the door with his fists. He called, "Hey, anybody there?" Did he really expect an answer? I had forgotten to switch off the lights. He must have been able to see that somebody was in the apartment. Why had I chosen an apartment with so many windows? I loved to have light, but I could see that the windows were a safety issue when I bought the apartment. I just did not want my life to be controlled by my father.

"Alexandra. I will call her. She may have a solution," I replied. I knew that Alexandra, my friend in Switzerland, would calm me down. She always knew a good solution. I dialed her number.

"Yes?"

"My father has found me. He is at my door," I said. I was sobbing. I heard how she took a deep breath.

Then she said, "God, why is this happening now? You have been through so much in the past few months."

She was right. In the past five months, my life had taken more than the usual twists and turns: I had quit my job. I had made plans to move to Spain. I had gotten a new job in that country. And I had broken up—for the third and last time—with the man who once had seemed to be my true love.

And now my father stood at my door. It seemed like the worst nightmare. I did not know what to say to Alexandra. I just wanted my father to stop pursuing me. I wanted him to respect me.

Alexandra had an idea: "You should call Silke. She will help you." Silke was our former colleague. I had not spoken to her during the past three years after I had changed jobs and she had given birth. I knew that she was now back at work. Silke was tall and I had always felt protected with her.

"Thank you. I'll do that." I called Silke. She answered the phone.

"Silke, it's me, Natalie. My father has found me and is at my door." I knew that she would understand.

She simply replied, "OK. I'll be at your place in an hour." I felt grateful for my friends. Suddenly, I knew that I was not alone anymore. Now there were people who took care of me.

Tim replied to my message. He knew about my past. I didn't need to explain anything. He gave me the phone number of an organization for victims of violence. I phoned them and explained what had happened and how my body was reacting. I felt that I had lost control of my arms and legs.

"You are in shock. You need to get up and drink a lot of water. Tomorrow, you have to call the police," a lady's voice explained. I assumed that she did not tell me to call the police immediately because my father had not threatened me in so many words and he did not appear to have a weapon. I thanked her and hung up. Then I sat on my bed for a moment and listened. Was my father still banging on the door? The noise seemed to have stopped. I wondered whether he was standing at the door in the darkness. I wasn't eager to find out. Slowly, like a snail, I got up, went into the kitchen with shaky steps, and got a glass of water. Then I went out on the terrace, where I grabbed a chair, sat down in the chilly air, and looked at the November sky. It was clear and black, with some brilliant stars. I just sat there, motionless, smoking one cigarette after another and waiting for Silke to arrive. My complete body was shaking. About an hour later, my bell rang once more. This time, I answered the buzzer: "Who is it?"

"It's me, Silke."

I pushed the door opener, and moments later, Silke appeared at my door. Tall and fearless as always, she just put her arms around me and hugged me.

During the past few years, I had come to accept my father's unwanted letters as part of my reality. After the victims department of the police had granted me a secret address years earlier, I thought that I had done all I could to protect myself. I wanted to live my life without being unduly influenced by an apprehension that my father might show up at my door. Even though I had feared it, I had never actually expected that my father would be able to find me.

The next morning, I phoned the victims department of the police. A female police officer answered the phone. I explained to her that I had already been there to apply for a secret address and that my father had now found me. She just listened to my words. I said, "I just need two weeks. By then I'll be in Spain. I just want my freedom." I was crying.

Then she said, "OK. I propose this: I can phone your father and talk to him. I'll also phone the police station that is closest to your house, so that you can call them if he returns. I'll phone you back as soon as I have done this. Is this OK for you?"

She wanted to talk to him. What if she next told me that he had a right to see me, to talk to me? What if she told me the same thing my father had told me: that I was wrong and that I had to honor my father? Didn't I have the right to be honored as a child? What if she told me that my father was a wonderful father? The self-doubts exploded in my head and didn't matter anymore. I needed help and so I answered, "Sure. Thank you."

I sat in my apartment on the steps that led to the terrace, feeling like a bird in a cage. I had felt so secure in my apartment, and the security had been an illusion. I did not know whether my father was waiting for me at the door. Did a father have the right to pursue a daughter if she told him not to? *No.*

I thought not but sometimes I felt that the voice of society said that I was obliged to have contact with him. Could it really be like that? Could it really be that he could pursue me and my sister all our lives with his cards and his visits?

Two hours later, I had to leave my house to organize my move. I looked out at the street. My red Mini Cooper stood on the road. I had to leave the protection of my apartment. I called Tim to ask whether he could help me get into my car. He suggested that

I text him once I was in the car. If I didn't do it, he would call the police. With this protection, I left my apartment with shaky knees, went down the stairs, left the house, and opened my car. I held my mobile in my hand as my protection. The street was empty. I drove to the subway station. For many years, I had tried to erase my father from my life and to ignore this threat. I couldn't do it anymore.

I arrived at the subway station and was just walking by the yellow walls of the cemetery when my phone rang. It was an unknown number. *It must be the police officer from the victims department.*

"Yes," I said, feeling vulnerable. What would she say to me? That my father was the best father in the world? That I had no right to cut off contact with him?

"I have talked to your father," she said.

I took a breath. Suddenly, he was so close, so present. Would this game of manipulation continue?

"He told me that he has paid for you all your life and that he has the right to see you. He also told me that if you want to inherit anything, you have to have contact with him. He wants to talk to you. How do you see this?"

An unstoppable flood of tears poured out of my eyes. I was in the middle of the street, and I could not hold them back. I did not care anymore what people might think. I just cried and answered, "No, no, I do not want his money. I do not want to talk to him." I feared her answer. Would she force me to? I wasn't sure. I felt like the little girl who had to go see her father, whether she wanted to or not. My mother's words rang in my ears: *He is your father. You have to accept him as he is.*

The police officer replied, "I understand and I will tell him so. I just want to add something. I have many years of experience with victims of violence. I have talked to your father, and I know that you have every reason to fear him. There is no need for you to tell me what actually happened in your childhood. I just have to tell you that you can also go to court."

I had not expected this. For the first time in my life, somebody outside my family who had spoken to my father had confirmed my truth about him. The inner wall of self-doubt and guilt that I had carried around broke. He was as he was, and I had the right to say no. My tears were partly pain and partly relief. Words couldn't express how grateful I was to the police officer. I did not want to go to court. It did not matter anymore. I couldn't change the past; I just wanted to make my peace with my past. I wanted to heal my soul.

So I answered, "Thank you for your help. I don't want to go to court. In two weeks I will be in Spain, and then I want to find my freedom." She said OK and that I should call her if I needed anything. She hung up. I leaned against the yellow wall of the cemetery while tears ran down my face. Above my head, I could see a gray sky shimmering through the dark brown branches, which had only a few remaining yellow-brown leaves. It was only when my father had confronted me that I could see the extent of my own fear, which I had always hidden to protect myself. Now I was able to embrace the full, frightening truth about my father. I had tried to see him through rose-colored glasses for so long. I allowed my tears to flow; they cleansed my soul and washed away the pain, shame, and guilt.

That evening, I returned home and rang my neighbor's bell. I told her that I was estranged from my father and did not want contact with him, but he had found me. I asked her to call the police if she heard strange noises. I told her that I would move to Spain in two weeks and that she should not tell anybody where I was. That evening, I overcame my fear and faced the reality that my father was violating my boundaries. I did not care anymore what others might think about me. Nobody's parents were perfect. So who had a right to judge me?

Two weeks after the unexpected visit of my father, I moved to Barcelona with my two cats. My friend Cornelia helped me make the move.

PART THREE
True Healing

The soul always knows what to do to heal itself.
The challenge is to silence the mind.

—Caroline Myss

I Fulfill My Yearning for Love

When I moved to Barcelona, I spent my weekends walking through the city, enjoying the colorful buildings and the impressive blue sky, or I sat on the beach, pondering the seeming infinity of the sea and the millions of opportunities that life offered.

On a full-moon, slightly chilly night in January, I sat on the balcony of my apartment. My spine rested against an iron fence, and my left hand was on my knees while I held my cigarette in my right hand. The moon shone brightly at the end of the Calle de la Luna. Street of the Moon—a wonderful name for my first home in Barcelona. I looked up at the sky and puffed on my cigarette.

From a distance, I could hear Michael Jackson's "I Just Can't Stop Loving You," which some neighbor played loudly. I felt a longing that maybe one day somebody would say this to me. And there was still this judging inner voice that said, *You are not lovable.* I still could not imagine that it would happen.

I had played Russian roulette with my heart when I returned to Sam after he had told me for the first time that he did not see a future with me. I hadn't saved him. Instead, my heart was left with a wound so deep that words could hardly describe it. Why was the wound so deep? My thoughts wandered. Maybe it was so deep because of the confusing messages I had received from him. Maybe it was because of the hurtful dynamic that I had lived: we would spend a wonderful day together, and then he would leave me. Maybe it was because I had ignored my inner knowing, which had told me that a relationship with him was not possible. Now I had my clarity again, and my broken heart would heal one day.

Why had I allowed hope to blind me? My rational mind judged me. But my heart said, *What is wrong with hoping? Nothing.* Without hope, I would never have started a new relationship. Had I been naive? Had I had sex with him too early? When was the right time to have sex with a man? Had he stayed with me only for sex? I shuddered. Maybe I should have waited longer. *But really, when do you have security? There is no security when you love somebody.* I just felt that I had hurt my own dignity and that I had disrespected my body. I was not a woman to have sex with a man without a commitment. But who knows in the beginning how a story will end?

I had given him one year to decide whether he wanted to have a relationship with me. One year was enough. And for one year, I had hoped that we could make it. Hope always dies last, but letting it go opens up the possibility of healing. I had tried to save Sam from his loneliness, from his disconnection from all human beings. Sam had never wanted to be saved. He had never asked for help. And anyway, I couldn't save my partner; I could save only myself.

Now I wanted to heal my wounds and prepare myself to have the relationship I wanted. I closed my eyes and imagined Sam in front of me. I looked into his dark brown eyes and told him, "I am very sorry. It is a pity that it was not possible. I will always carry you in my heart." I put my hand on my heart. It was time to let him go forever.

The melody of "I Just Can't Stop Loving You" faded away. The silence of the night surrounded me. My relationships seemed to be a long list of errors. I wanted to find a partner who was close to me, who loved me for being myself, and who could make a commitment to me. I just had to change myself to attract what I wanted. I took the last puff of the cigarette and looked up at the moon. Silently, I prayed for help.

After Sam and I broke up, I blamed myself for the failure of the relationship and withdrew from the world and men. I felt too ashamed. Despite the fact that I longed for a relationship, I condemned any dream of having one as neediness. Instead, I concentrated on my independence. I had to prove to myself that I did not need a man. For nearly two years, I focused on my own healing.

Two weeks after my night on the balcony, I returned to Munich for a weekend to do my first family constellation. My mother's side showed up. I saw the repetitive pattern of the women in my family, who shut down their emotions and rejected men. My mother's representative stood there alone; she did not allow anybody to come closer. She was not able to look at my father's representative. This pattern repeated itself throughout generations. After the constellation, I asked Renate what the next step would be. "Heal your inner child," she said.

I had never heard about my inner child before, so I went into a bookstore the next day and bought a book about it. Back in Barcelona, I sat down on my red and orange sofa to read the book and work through the exercises. It proposed that I should become a loving adult for the child who resided within me, wounded by my childhood experiences. How could I be a good and loving parent without having experienced good and loving parenting? I only knew how it shouldn't be. I sighed. Yet there was this inner yearning, this dream of how it should have been. I had my doubts, yet I decided to learn to be a good and loving parent. I sat down and defined my own concept of a loving parent.

Then the book proposed that I write an adoption letter to my inner child. I wrote this:

Dear Natalie,

I know that I have ignored you for a long time, and I am sorry for this. Now I want to protect you, and I want to be the loving parent that you never had in childhood. I want to communicate with you and understand your world. I will make mistakes but I will learn to be a good parent. Please have patience with me. From today on, I will protect you and I will take care of you. You are no longer alone, because I will stay with you for the rest of your life.

I had chosen a stuffed animal to connect with her. It was a soft gray rhino, a present from a friend who lived in Los Angeles. When I had finished with the letter, I took the soft rhino into my arms and read it aloud. Later, I just sat down and imagined that I hugged myself as a little child. I pinned the letter on the wall of the bedroom to remind myself of my intention.

In the beginning, nothing happened. I just kept hugging the rhino whenever I felt lonely or sad. Deep in my heart, I set the intention to connect and communicate with my inner little girl.

Three months later, it was time to move again. I had found an apartment in El Born, about twenty minutes away. I stood in my old apartment in El Raval, a quarter in Ciutat Vella, the old town in the heart of Barcelona. It was Easter Sunday and the sun was shining. My cats were already packed in their transport boxes. They meowed in high-pitched voices, not knowing where they would end up. I looked around the small furnished apartment, which had been my first home in Barcelona. I silently said good-bye and thank you to its warm yellow walls, colorful sofa, and small balcony.

Then I put my cats on my shoulders, slightly nervous about their safe arrival. "Just relax, everything is OK," I said to myself and my cats. I could make out Thor's eyes, which were deeply black and staring at me, full of panic. I left the apartment and went down the staircase. When I stepped onto the cobblestone street, the warm rays of the spring sun hit my face. The sky was deeply blue with some white clouds. I looked up and saw the balconies, where the multicolored clothes of my neighbors were hung to dry; next to them, I could see some green leaves from the plants that had found their way through the iron bars surrounding the balconies.

I walked silently down the streets and through the narrow alleys of El Raval in the direction of Las Ramblas, one of Barcelona's most famous streets. When I got to Las Ramblas, the pedestrian mall was filled with the noise of hundreds of voices speaking all kinds of languages. The sun was now shining through the fresh green leaves of the huge trees, and the stands sold colorful flowers. I made my slalom through the people walking and loitering on the road. Loki looked at me with big eyes through the grill of her box. I was laughing inside: How many people had carried their cats on Las Ramblas before? Why was I so stubborn that I did not want to take a cab? Why was it so important for me to walk it all by myself? I just did what felt right for me.

My shoulders started to hurt while I continued my walk through Calle Ferran and into the Gótico, passing bars, restaurants, and cafés, as well as Plaza St. Jaume, where the city hall was. I crossed Via Laietana, as always full of traffic, and I caught a glimpse of the masts of the sailboats that lay in Port Vell, the old harbor. Finally, I arrived at my new apartment, which was on a narrow street, with not much distance between me and my neighbors on the other side of the street. My furniture from Munich had arrived just the week before. Now, with my cats, it would become my new home. Somehow, they understood that we had arrived and started to scratch at the doors of their boxes. I opened the doors and they started exploring the apartment, fearful but curious. Soon, they recognized the old furniture and relaxed.

I sat down on a wooden box and massaged my shoulders. I felt small and young. I was tired. Most of all, I felt happy. I looked at the door. I remembered when I had seen my father through the peephole of my door in Munich. I was now in Spain, and in Spain there were no names next to the bells. I had checked this already in summer 2008. My father could not ring my bell here. I did not want to have a secret address anymore. I did not want to live in fear anymore that he might find me. How many years had I hidden? How many years had I feared him? How many years had I struggled to be free? As far as I could remember, all my life. But now—now I was free. I felt it in my body. I was far away and free. It seemed unbelievable. Tears started running down my face. How long had I waited for this feeling? I was free. I was safe. I had never felt safe before in my life.

Suddenly, a small, high-pitched voice inside me spoke: *Finally, you have kept your promise. You have kept me waiting for such a long time. Finally, you've moved to a different country.* My inner child really talked to me. I felt that I had made myself this promise as a small child. I had always wanted to go away, but always had seen other people's wishes as more important than my own. First, there was my grandfather; then there was Paolo. For many years, I had ignored just how important that step was for me.

I responded silently to my inner child: *I'm sorry that I waited so long to do this. I'm sorry that I ignored you for so long. I'm glad that I have finally done it.* Tears flowed down my face, tears that washed away the sadness and pain of what I had experienced as a child and tears of gratitude and joy for where I was right now. My heart filled with comfort and warmth and became lighter. Finally, I had made it, alone. I had given up everything—and I had won myself. I was on the road that would lead me to freedom.

Connecting with my inner child became a continuous process. Not only did I explore my childhood wounds, but I also allowed her to be a child again. I asked her in the morning what kinds of clothes she wanted to wear, what colors she liked. She loved to draw and dance, so I did those things. As time passed, she became more and more alive. This loving, creative approach also helped me later on, when I decided to stop smoking.

One year later, I asked her how she had experienced her childhood, and she painted a picture that was black with four orange flashes. Then I asked her how she felt right now, and she painted a picture consisting of a yellow background and bands in all the colors of the rainbow dancing there. My heart as a loving parent filled with gratitude. I believe that now I can give myself the childhood I have always wanted. The connection with my inner child helped me to understand my needs and take responsibility for my feelings. The image of being a loving parent helped me to have a compassionate and loving view of myself.

Three years later, I wrote a poem to my inner child to acknowledge all that had happened in my life:

A child of three

Within me lives a child of three.

Three years old, she has lost her innocence.
Three years old, she has lost her smile.
Three years old, she has lost the shining in her eyes.
Three years old, she has lost hope.
Three years old, she has lost faith in humanity.
Three years old, she has lost love.
Three years old, she has lost her connection to the
    world.
Three years old, she has lost her life.
Three years old, she has lost a piece of her soul.

Within me lives a child of three.

Three years old, she has learned that men are evil.
Three years old, she has learned that sex is cruel and
  dirty.
Three years old, she has learned that hate exists.
Three years old, she has learned that life is suffering.
Three years old, she has learned that the world is dark.

Within me lives a child of three.

For years, she screamed silently in the darkness with
no one listening.
For years, she saw no colors.
For years, she feared life.
For years, she was more dead than alive.

Within me lives a child of three.

The wound in her heart was so deep that words could
hardly describe it.
The pain was so great that words could hardly express it.

Within me lives a child of three.
She has survived all that.

One day, I was able to see her in her dark and cold corner.
One day, I was able to listen to her.
One day, I was able to love her as she is.
One day, I was able to care for her.
One day, I was able to protect her.
One day, I was able to give her the love she needed.
One day, I was able to play with her.
One day, I was able to hug her.
One day, I was able to feel her pain.
One day, I was able to heal her pain.

Within me lives a child of three.

Now she has the parent she always wished for.
Now she speaks again.
Now she has faith again.
Now she feels again.
Now she smiles again.
Now she sees the world in bright colors again.
Now she hopes again.
Now she believes in miracles again.
Now she plays again.
Now she is able to trust again.
Now she is able to love again.

I have my love again.
I have my life again.
I have my soul again.

I felt proud of my inner child, and I was grateful that she had survived. The expression "It's never too late to have a happy childhood" is true. My inner child just needed me to make it a reality.

In 2010, I started my coaching training in Barcelona. I used this training to change my negative relationship patterns, such as my fear of rejection, my withdrawal and self-abandonment during conflict, and my fear of intimacy. I questioned the truth of my negative beliefs about myself and changed them into positive ones. One belief was "Everyone else is better than me in every way"; another one was "I am not lovable." Every morning, I told myself, "I am good the way I am" and "I am lovable."

I connected with my inner parts and explored them to understand their needs.

Sometimes my inner needs were so contradictory that I didn't know how to address them, so I had a coaching session a year later via Skype in my apartment in Barcelona. I wanted to resolve my inner conflict: Is having a relationship neediness?

My coach proposed that I talk to my inner parts that were involved in this game. I saw my essence as a happy snail with a colorful house who crawled calmly through the world; nothing could shock her.

Then there was my independent part, a galloping horse. I liked her because she had courage and would overcome any obstacle in her way. Yet when she encountered problems, she could turn into an unruly wild horse who would strike out and run away. I remembered the emails I had sent to Sam that were full of blame and anger. Then I felt ashamed of her. Yet without a partner, she would never become unruly. She felt safe when she was single.

And then there was a part of me that I rejected, even hated. This was a woman who wanted to be nice to people and always ended up pleasing too much. For a year, I had tried to find the benefit of this part but could not. To me, she was a gray mouse, a worthless nothing. It was her fault that I had adapted too much to the expectations of my partners, her fault that I had stayed too long in manipulative relationships. I had not yet come to terms with this part of myself. Why had I been so submissive? Why hadn't I seen earlier that I was disrespecting my own limits?

My coach told me to start with my independent part, so I searched in the room for her. He asked me. "How does she feel?"

I closed my eyes and connected with my body. Then I said, "She feels fine. She does what she wants. She does not like the gray mouse; she adapts too much to other people."

Then he asked me, "What animal would represent her?"

I waited for a moment and then said, "A bird with powerful, bright colors." The picture of the galloping horse had changed into a bird that was flying in the air.

Then he asked me to look for another spot. There, I could connect with the adapting part. I chose a place far away from the independent one. He asked me what she felt. Suddenly, I felt a deep sorrow inside and said, "She is sad. She does not feel seen by the other parts. She also feels guilty for the mistakes in the past. She wants to have a partner to love and knows that the independent part will not allow her to do so. She feels sorry that she adapted so much in the past." Suddenly, I felt guilty for having treated her so badly.

I saw the little child in her, who knew only manipulative relationships. My heart filled with compassion. She had not known any better.

My coach asked what it would feel like if I could touch her.

I closed my eyes and said, "She feels like velvet and silk. And she invites me to touch her." That moment, I became aware that this part helped me to connect with other people. So she was precious to me because of that and because she yearned to have a good relationship, to share her life with somebody. The independent part always forgot about other people. Tears welled up in my eyes. This was a relief. I took a breath.

My coach asked what animal I saw in her. I waited a moment and then saw a lotus flower. Long ago, I had read about the lotus flower. It has its roots in the dirt and mud, yet it grows and becomes a beautiful flower. It had been a comforting metaphor for my life. I grew up in the darkness and wanted to transform myself into a flower. Relieved to have found a positive picture for her, I said, "I can't see any animal but I see a flower." I felt much better.

After the session ended, I sat outside on my balcony and thought about what had happened. In the past two years, I had judged my desire to have a relationship as neediness. Suddenly, I saw that each part had its good side and its bad side. My bird could become too independent and egotistical and forget about other people, yet it would always help me have the courage to overcome a crisis. My flower part would connect me with other people, and in case she adapted too much, the bird could take some of her pollen to the snail, so the flower and the snail could connect. It was all about finding the right balance. One hour after the session, I received an email from my coach.

He wrote, "Now imagine yourself as a bird flying in the sky, holding a fragile flower in its beak, with the snail riding on its back." When I saw his words, I got a vivid picture in my mind's eye. I smiled. Suddenly, the three parts I had fought with for the past two years came together like the pieces of a puzzle. They all made sense and they all helped me be the person I am. I did not want a relationship out of neediness. I wanted a relationship so that I could share my love. I smiled. I knew that with this perspective, a relationship would enrich my life.

Two weeks later, my coach emailed me to ask how I wanted to celebrate the launch of my website. I replied that what I really wanted to do did not yet exist.

"What if the impossible were possible?" came his response.

I sighed, sat down at my computer, and wrote this:

"I go with my partner to a small restaurant on the beach that has very good and simple food, a mixture of Mediterranean and Asian. We sit on the terrace at a table with candlelight; the sky is full of stars and the moon is full. We look at each other with brilliant eyes, talking, laughing, and holding hands. After dinner, we have mochas with cardamom. Later, we stroll to the beach and sit on the sand, feeling the breeze on our faces and the sand under our feet. The full moon is mirrored in the sea. With my head on his shoulder, we dream about our future, enjoying being together and connecting without talking. From a distance, we hear our song—maybe we dance. Still later, we walk through the city, maybe eating crepes with dark chocolate, and we return home with smiles on our faces and feeling very happy."

I pushed the Send button with tears in my eyes. I had committed to my dream. I had openly said that I wanted a relationship again. I would take the risk again to get to know men and meet the right man for me. Even though I was happy being single, fulfilling this dream would make my life even happier. I sighed and knew that one day my dream would come true. The Universe would answer.

Exploring my inner parts helped me discover my needs. It was a continuous process and the relationship between my inner parts and myself changed over time. The more I saw them with compassion, the more I could use them for my highest good and the more they supported my dreams.

Meanwhile, I learned to distinguish between an abusive relationship and a loving relationship. I read books that confirmed my own experiences. Then I attended the Organization and Relationship Systems Coaching curriculum to become a coach of relationships and teams, where I found new perspectives and tools that help to create and maintain a healthy relationship. It was a deeply gratifying experience, because I saw that creative solutions in relationships were always possible and that there was no need to end up in a blind alley. Step by step, I put together my own ideas about a healthy relationship and what type of relationship I needed.

In October 2012, I still had some doubts about myself. Dr. Mueller's words lingered in my mind: "You are complicated. You will always find complicated men." I needed help to believe in my own definition of my desired relationship. I wanted to make sure that it was a healthy relationship, free of manipulation. I wanted to make sure that it wasn't complicated. I had a session with Sofia, my instructor for family constellations. She was a woman in her fifties with short hair and blue eyes. She was quite energetic but also calm and loving. I trusted Sofia and I knew that she was the right person to consult.

In our first session, she said, "Natalie, the right man for you is out there. He lives and breathes. You just have to change your focus. How will the Universe know who to carry to you if you don't tell it specifically, with all the details?"

I had never dared to write down more than a vague description, because I feared that I would never find a suitable man. To a certain extent, I still saw myself as a strange person who would not fit well with anybody. Sofia continued: "I want you to describe in detail what you need in a relationship. It's not enough to say that you want respect. Describe what *respect* means to you. Describe how much you want to give to your partner—how much time you have for the relationship, your business, and yourself. If not, you'll always fear that you'll lose your freedom."

I agreed. Over the next five weeks, I wrote down everything. For the first time in my life, I allowed myself to describe what I really wanted and needed. It was free of any conditioning, either from my childhood or my past relationships. It included all I had learned over the past few years about myself and about relationships.

Five weeks later, I sat in front of Sofia, holding five pages in my hands. There was still a tiny voice within that was afraid to share my words, that was afraid to be judged. My hands were shaking slightly.

She looked at me calmly and said, "Before we start, I want to place a chair for your invisible companion at your side, your guardian angel. I feel that he is accompanying you, and I want him to have a seat."

I nodded.

She got up, grabbed a chair, and put it by my side. I felt his protection. Then she sat down again. The room was silent.

I looked at the five pages in my hands, which described my ideal relationship. This time, I jettisoned all my doubts and limiting beliefs about not finding this man. It was a gesture of self-respect, the best gift that I could give myself.

I started reading: "He is attractive, athletic, and well built. He has a positive attitude toward life and is fully alive. Professionally, he is successful and has a good balance between time for work, time for himself, for our relationship, for family, and for friends."

Sofia stopped me and said, "Natalie, this is for you. Take your time and read it patiently."

I nodded. I had noticed while I wrote my list how it transformed me on an emotional level. Each time I wrote down an attribute of this man that none of my boyfriends had possessed, I let go of old pain. The bad memory was discarded while the dream became real.

I resumed reading: "He has a healthy self-respect, loves himself, and is connected with his inner child. He has good and deep friendships. He is honest and speaks his opinions, thoughts, and feelings openly. He has learned from the experience that life has brought him. He has forgiven his ex-partners and either is friends with them or speaks well of them. He knows what he has learned from the relationships and in what ways they were good for him."

My heart opened up, thinking about this man and being with him.

"He is grateful for what he has. He does what he says and says what he does. He knows what he wants and who he is. I feel safe and relaxed with him, and I perceive him as being as clear and predictable as a deep lake with stones that you can see on the bottom."

Some tears coursed down my cheeks to let go of the hurt of past relationships.

"He loves nature and protects nature and animals. He does not waste resources, and he respects the Earth. He loves cats and plays frequently with my cats. The cats are allowed to sleep in our bed, and he is relaxed about the cat hair."

Finally, I had accepted that I needed a partner who loved animals. I had let go of the struggle that I had with Paolo about the cats. It was such a relief! I continued: "He loves the sea and likes to be out in nature. He enjoys walking, hiking, or just sitting by the sea and looking silently at the ocean. He communicates his feelings clearly and straightforwardly or by using creative language and metaphors. He has goals. He wants to grow in life and has the intention to live free from fear. He assumes responsibility for his own thoughts, feelings, and behavior. He lives according to his values, which are based on Buddhist principles, but seeks his own truth and follows it. He defines his own rules with flexibility. He has a good sense of humor and can laugh at himself. I see him as a majestic old tree with new green leaves and deep roots.

"My family of origin and my story are in his heart, and he is at peace with his own family."

Here I needed to pause to swallow a big ball of pain in my throat. A man who would accept my story and my family as I did—that was a wonderful thought. I took a breath and picked up where I had left off: "He trusts me and I trust him. We dream of spending our lives together, and we know that there is no guarantee of success; the success of our relationship depends on the two of us. This way, our relationship is always fresh, and we both focus on keeping it alive. We will know that our relationship is a forever relationship only when we look back on our common path at the end of our lives while holding hands and smiling, knowing that it is good as it is. We know that we are fine without the other, so we have chosen—not needed—the relationship. Our bond is made up of our love, our shared dreams, and our commitment. Our relationship is constantly flowing and changing as we change; sometimes it is a calm and deep stream, and other times, it is a fresh and alive mountain creek."

I became more secure in my reading, even though I did not dare look up at Sofia. I imagined that I read it to myself with all the invisible powers as witness to what I really needed. The ability to write and read my story had helped to heal my past; now I used this ability to help create my desired future. I continued: "We like to spend time together and enjoy our moments together. In the evening, we sit together, usually in the candlelight, with my head leaning on his shoulder. He puts an arm around my shoulder, and we talk about the day, what moved us, and what we want to achieve the next day. Or we go for a walk and look at the stars. In these moments, I feel a deep connection with him.

"The daily chores, such as cleaning, cooking, and shopping, we split evenly. We alternate the cooking, and usually we make healthy, quick, and easy dishes, but every now and then we cook together and create a feast from what we have in the fridge. We enjoy eating our meals slowly and use the time to talk and laugh a lot. It's perfectly OK with him that I'm a vegetarian; if he wants meat, he cooks it himself. It's also perfectly OK with him that I eat only small amounts and do not drink alcohol."

I continued, "Overall, he drinks alcohol moderately, as he enjoys a good glass of wine or a cocktail in a bar. During the week, he does not drink alcohol at all.

"In the house, he needs a creative chaos, the way I do. And, like me, he cleans it up periodically. He also likes to let go of all that he no longer needs. With him, I feel light as a feather, motivated, and cheerful like a rippling creek.

"Our house is open to our friends, who spend the weekend with us or have dinner with us at home. Sometimes he meets up with his friends without me, and sometimes I do the same. We both know that the other one's friends are important.

"We speak lovingly about our relationship. When we talk with strangers, that person can immediately perceive the love, affection, and respect we feel for each other. I can feel the love in my eyes when I tell others with strength and confidence that he is the man in my life.

"At least every second Saturday, we take time only for our-selves (and our children), putting our work aside. In the winter, we go for long walks on the beach. In the summer, we go for hikes in the mountains, usually with the children and some-times just the two of us. Every now and then, we go to the mov-ies, an art exhibit, or a concert. I feel light and happy by his side.

"We usually take simple and cozy vacations in nature, mostly in apartments or in a tent. I feel closely connected to him and am in harmony with him, and I enjoy every moment with him.

Sometimes we take a weekend trip, and sometimes I go alone with a female friend or he with a male friend.

"I like to dance with him. Sometimes we are very close and wrapped tightly together, and sometimes we look at each other from afar, playing with the distance but always sensing our invisible bond of attraction. If we spend a few days apart, our reunion is great, and we enjoy listening to each other's stories and experiences.

"My partner gives me space for my professional projects, whether they are my trainings and workshops to help my clients connect with their essence and have healthy relationships, my writing, or my project in India. He backs me up in stressful moments, and I do the same for him. We inspire and motivate each other. He allows me my own area in our house, where I can write and work, and he gives me the time I need to be alone. We are important advisers for each other. I feel respected, safe, supported, and motivated. In the relationship, I feel like a bird who flies out happily into the world and always likes to return to our cozy nest, knowing that I bring some good news for the nest that will make it even more cozy and happy.

"If one partner opens his or her heart or shows a glimpse of his or her soul, we know that the other will treat this with care and love. He listens to me, understands what I say, and asks questions—and I do the same. If I say no, then he respects this. I do the same. He communicates clearly and understandably his opinions and his truth. He remembers my words and his words. Like me, he can forgive and ask for forgiveness. He can say that he is sorry and can admit to his mistakes. He chooses his words carefully because he understands their power. If there is a misunderstanding, one of us will communicate with the other. If we have a conflict, we strive to respect the boundaries of the other and to stop a heated discussion before it escalates; we both take the time to cool off. Whenever we have an argument, we hug in reconciliation. We strive to reconcile before we lie down to sleep.

"He is affectionate and places great value on hugs and cuddling. We enjoy touching each other, even if only briefly—a gentle brush of the arm, shoulder, or face, a quick kiss, or an intimate embrace. We always feel just the way we did when we first fell in love: the butterflies in the stomach always remain. We walk through the streets holding hands, and feeling his touch gives me positive energy and warmth. I feel feminine and strong, and his touch always feels comfortable on my skin. Through his touch, I feel deeply connected to him."

I took a break. Tears pricked my eyes. In my childhood, I had experienced my father's hugs as invasive and back-breaking and the kisses of my stepfather as disgusting; now all this negativity was changed and I could allow myself just to enjoy the physical touch of a man. I had needed many years to find out that my love language is touch. I have to feel my partner. Nothing else connects me so deeply with my partner.

"We have great sex and laugh when we make love. I feel relaxed, I trust him, and I can let myself go. Faithfulness in the relationship is important to both of us. I have positive energy, and deep in my gut I jump for joy. I feel that I have air to breathe. My inner child feels well. She knows that she can just be herself and that she can be crazy if she wants to, and then he will laugh with her."

I paused while a tear coursed down my cheek. A man with whom my inner child could relax: what a relief that would be! I looked up and said to Sofia, "The next part is about children. I am thirty-nine and I probably won't have children. But I wanted to write it down, just to honor my wish."

I resumed reading: "We have at least one child together, and it's perfectly OK if he has children from a previous relationship. He is a good father and has a close and cordial relationship with the children. He plays with the children and teaches them to be brave—to bounce back from a mistake—and he encourages them to develop freely. The children know that they can explore the world with curious eyes while he always stands behind them to protect them. No matter what happens, he is always there for them; even if they make a mistake, he will always love them with all his heart. He climbs around with them on trees and on rocks and plays team sports with them. He is aware of his responsibilities as a father, and if a child does not feel well, he knows that this may have something to do with us. Together, we will work to solve it so that our child gets better. Sometimes when I see him with the children, tears come to my eyes because I am so grateful that the children have such a wonderful father."

The room was silent. I had written down all that I had learned in twenty years about relationships. I had shared my dream. I sat on the chair and swallowed my tears and the lump in my throat. I had not had this kind of father, yet I had learned what a good father is. I had never experienced a healthy relationship, yet I had learned what a relationship should be.

After some moments, I was able to look up into Sofia's eyes. We sat there in silence. Did I see a tear in her eye? She said, "That was a wonderful description. You thought about everything. There is a balance between give and take."

I responded, "But that is how a relationship should be."

She made a gesture at the window and said, "And you know how many people out there would tell you something different, don't you?"

I looked at her. Yes, I knew that there was still much suffering in relationships. But I didn't understand why. During the past four years, I had found solutions for any relationship problem. I knew that a positive relationship is possible; it requires only the willingness of the two people involved, goals in common, and the ability of each partner to take responsibility for his or her own emotions, needs, and dreams. True love is not so difficult when the rewards are considered, but it does take practice. Didn't the skeptics about romance see what they were missing? I sighed. I was not responsible for other people's lives, just for mine. And I had transformed it.

Defining my dreams helped me to stay focused and point my energy in the right direction. It also helped me to define a reality that I had never really experienced. It let me drop most of the conditioning from my past and allowed me to define what I needed. Years ago, my past had shaped my reality; now I intended to shape my reality by defining my dreams and focusing on what I wanted and needed. I now had my own dreamer's compass to guide me.

I now rely on myself to fulfill my yearning for love. I have a compassionate and loving relationship with myself, and I take care of my feelings, needs, and dreams. I believe that I have to love myself in order to be able to give and receive love. I will always continue to deepen my relationship with myself because love has no limits. I love my partner while I love myself. That is the balance a healthy relationship needs. The exterior world is a mirror of a person's interior world. If I respect myself, my values, my principles, and my needs, my partner will respect me. Loving myself also protects me so that I will not remain in a relationship that is abusive or manipulative.

I Transform My Story

Another part of my healing process was transforming my story. I chose the means that I felt was correct for me, allowing my intuition to guide me.

In April 2011, I did a constellation to confront the sexual violence in my past. It was a sunny day in Barcelona. I sat on a chair in a circle of twelve women in a spacious and light-filled room in a basement in Gràcia, a district in Barcelona. The facilitator of the constellation, Carmen, sat by my side. I had gotten to know her seven months earlier, when I went to her constellation group with her sister, who had been my classmate in my coaching group. I had observed that she treated her clients with respect and warmth, not judgment, while maintaining a safe environment. She had long, dark, curly hair and vivid brown eyes. She had an energy of joy, calm, and security. I knew that I could trust her.

Today, I wanted to constellate the violence in my family, and I wanted to be sure that my family wasn't judged. I sat on a chair, noticing how heavy my body felt. I could hardly breathe. Carmen asked me to give her some details, so I said, "In my childhood, violence and abuse happened. I want to liberate them." Tears sprang to my eyes while I revealed my family's story. I could hardly talk; it was as though all the pain of my childhood had suddenly come up again.

Carmen pushed her chair a bit closer to me and laid her hand on my back. She said quietly, "Natalie, breathe. Just breathe." I tried to do this. After some breaths, I calmed down.

Then she asked me to choose representatives for the violence and for myself. I did so. After some time, the person who represented me lay down on the floor. Carmen asked her what was going on, and she said, "It is a feeling of impotence. If I look at the violence, it is too much for me." I observed her and felt the pain in my body. Tears ran down my face. How well I understood her words. How well this image corresponded with my inner world. I had always felt that I had been thrown to the ground and pinned there while I was assaulted. All throughout my childhood, it was too much for me and overwhelmed me.

Carmen moved another inch closer and put an arm around my shoulders. She reminded me, "Breathe. Just breathe." Then she said, "Choose a representative for your parents." I nodded, got up, and chose a person to represent my parents. I positioned her in the circle. As soon as she entered the circle, the violence went to her. Suddenly, my representative could get up again. Carmen invited me to go to my representative, so I got up and stood by her side. We stood there, arm in arm, and looked at the other side of the room, where the representative of my parents stood together with the representative of the violence. I looked at both of them. The violence had accompanied me for so many years. It had been so close, so overwhelming. Carmen invited the representative of my parents to tell us that the parents were sorry, so she said, "I'm sorry."

The words reached me deep in my soul. How much I had yearned for those words. I had never dared to hope to hear it one day. I took a breath and a dam broke inside me, just as if the first protection wall that I had built around myself in my childhood had broken down. Tears rolled down my face, tears that washed away the pain of childhood. After a while, Carmen moved us toward the door of the room. She gestured toward the door and said, "Imagine that you have moved far away from what happened in the past and that here is the future." I stood there in front of the door while hugging my representative, and together we looked at the door. I imagined that I was looking at my future, and I saw how the brilliant daylight entered through the frosted glass, peacefully shimmering.

In that moment, I knew that every pain I had lived through was worth it, because those pains had led me to the place where I was able to see the light that was the future.

After the constellation, I went to a subway station, Joanic, just around the corner. I sat down on a bench and looked around. The place was surrounded by some medium-size apartment houses, and next to the benches were some small trees. The wood was dark and the trees were covered with many, many tiny dark pink flowers. I just sat there and breathed while seeing the beauty around me. My body felt moved in just the way that the ocean moves when the waves are high because of a heavy storm.

During the following months, I noticed subtle inner changes. Just as in the constellation, an inner part of me got up and was able to move again. I had more energy. Most of the shame and guilt went away, and the sexual abuse lost its horror. I became able to share this experience with others while feeling strong.

In May 2011, I saw Lisa Bloom at a coaching conference in Madrid. She was a storyteller and a coach. She was onstage on the last day of the conference and energized the tired atmosphere in the auditorium, bewitching the five hundred people in the audience when she started to tell a story. That day, she cast a spell on me. My intuition told me that I had to contact her and start working with her. And so I did.

First, I did her program to develop my marketing story. She asked me to write about the turning points in my life, and for the first time, I wrote about different experiences and shared them with Lisa. Never before had I shared with anybody the details of what had happened the day my mother died. I hadn't seen any point in doing so. Lisa helped me find an empowering way to tell my story. She helped me express myself and share my truth.

Writing about the turning points in my life helped get them out of my head and stop a painful cycle of reliving the experiences again and again. I became an observer of myself in the scenes and was able to put more of the necessary distance between the events and myself. It helped me to better understand what happened inside myself. It helped me to let go of part of the shame and guilt that still were connected to these scenes that I couldn't liberate by talking about them. Finally, it allowed me to put the events where they belonged—in the past.

Some months later, I started Lisa's program to become a story coach. During the program, I felt that it was time to share my story about my relationship with Sam. The relationship was a burden that was dragging me down. I wrote the story and did a session with Lisa where I read her the story:

"We were at a wonderful market, surrounded by booths selling colorful things from all over the world, the air filled with the smell of exotic food. I looked at the man at my side. I had achieved all I had dreamed of. My first date with this charming man—English, good looking, and witty—seemed as though it should be so wonderful, like a dream.

"Instead, I felt horrible and awkward and caged. I noticed this solid wall around me all the time. It put an unbearable pressure on me. When he drove me home, he tried to give me a kiss—and then it happened. I heard myself saying, 'This will never work out,' coldly and sharply. It was the voice of my fear. I pushed him away and just tried to get out of the situation. I felt this fear inside, dark, deep, and ice cold, telling me just to get out of there; otherwise, I would die. My inner child had taken control of me and was projecting all her anger and fears from her childhood on to this man. I was powerless and unable to stop it. And inside, my heart was crying.

"Somehow, we continued with a difficult relationship for a year, splitting up and starting again, never really able to communicate with each other. We hardly ever phoned each other. There was always this strong, solid wall between us, and I was unable to tear it down. I was his mirror and he was mine.

"Finally, I bought a book about the fear of commitment and how you can deal with it. I wanted to understand our dynamics. And I found in the book something I did not want to see: I had the same fear of relationships that my partner had. It made me feel small, like a loser. I had never wanted to be influenced so intensely by my childhood experiences. But I was.

"Once we broke up, I started working with myself and my inner child. For two years, I focused on changing this picture of myself by reading books, analyzing my past relationships to discern my patterns, and working to change them. For two years, I did not dare to date. I was too afraid that I would return to my old habits. When I was angry with myself, I told myself that wanting a relationship was just neediness. I told myself that I had to be independent.

"And then along came this man whom I did not notice at first. By some lucky circumstances, I could not avoid seeing him again. He was tall, brown haired, attractive. In the past, my inner child had feared tall men because of her childhood experience, but this time it was OK. My intuition told me that it was time to date again. So I dared to ask him out for coffee.

"After that, I had dinner with him on a Saturday evening. Later that evening, we went for a walk through the city. We just talked about ourselves. I felt well, relaxed, and connected with myself. I did not feel any wall around me. I said what I really wanted to say. I just was who I am. When we said good-bye, I was able to give him a hug and thank him for the nice evening. That evening, I did not run away for the first time in my life, and I achieved something important for me. And I knew I could repeat it anytime." I stopped. I was in tears.

After a pause, Lisa asked me, "Why are you so emotional?"

I answered that I felt so emotional because I was ashamed of my earlier behavior.

Lisa said, "Natalie, it is normal to have fears about your childhood experiences. The only thing that you have to do is forgive yourself."

Forgive myself: it seemed so difficult. I wanted to have a positive relationship, yet part of me still believed that I had chosen a destiny that made it impossible for me to achieve this. Forgive myself for my mistakes? It seemed to be an unattainable goal.

I sighed. Lisa was right. I had to forgive myself. I had taken responsibility for healing my childhood wounds. This was my responsibility as an adult. As a child, I had been innocent of blame and unable to heal my hurts. Silently, I reminded myself, *Now I have the ability to heal myself; in fact, I am the only person who can do so. In this way, I reclaim my power and find freedom. And this is a lifelong duty: I will continue to heal my emotional wounds, whether from the past or the present.*

Lisa said, "I want you to add to this story what you have learned from this. I feel that you should share the story with the group, if you want." I was afraid to share it with the group, yet I also knew that I had to do it to liberate my shame and to forgive myself.

The next day, I sat down and made a list of all that I had learned. I wrote down all the tools that I knew to improve relationships and the difference between abuse and true love. The fact that my friends regularly asked me for advice about their relationships let me know that I had profound knowledge about relationships. I had improved and deepened my friendships, and I had found a new circle of friends in Spain whom I loved very much. I sat with the paper. *What else do I need to do to prove to myself that I have left these problems behind?* I asked myself. *Nothing,* came the silent answer. I wasn't perfect, yet nobody is perfect. I would make mistakes. But that is normal and I would continue to learn and grow.

One week later, I shared my story with the group. This time,

I added my learnings: "My fear has transformed me, and now I work actively on my relationships, looking at every situation from the perspective of What can I learn from this? This helps me be authentic and not play games. And even though love has its limits—abuse or mistreatment mustn't be tolerated—I now see a relationship as something precious that should not be thrown away easily. It deserves constant attention. I need to work on myself continuously so that my partner and I can stay together. If I leave my partner and look for a new one without learning what I should learn from the situation, I will face the same problem—only with a different actor. I would just waste my time and would have to learn later what I could learn now.

"My fear helps me to stay curious and creative about finding the best way to relate to someone and not giving up easily. In the end, we all want to connect with other people, and connecting with others should give us positive energy and a lot of fun. It helps me to really live life and stay in the present.

"Stories can be powerful healers of our lives. We are all human and we all have our scars, our wounds, and our mistakes. What is important is how we deal with them, what we make out of them.

"For a long time, I saw my fear of relationships as my biggest mistake, and I was unable to forgive myself. By writing the story, the wound and the sense of failure get redefined and described differently. This time, I tell my story from a loving and compassionate point of view. This is the true healing."

When I had finished, the audience was still for a moment. *What do they think of me?* I dismissed this thought and told myself to calm down. *It's my story and I'll never be able to control other's people's thoughts or feelings.* I knew that I had done the right thing, even though it had required a lot of courage. I had taken a step forward in not judging myself but loving and accepting myself as I am.

The next day, a colleague asked me to send her my story. She wanted to share it with a client. I was surprised. I had never expected that anybody would regard my story as a tool to help other people.

In the end, I found that writing and sharing my story allowed me to reclaim my power and to be honest and authentic.

The storytelling and coaching program continued via Skype, and a couple of weeks later, I stood in front of my computer with the Skype program open. It was already dark outside, and a heater was next to my chair, keeping me warm. Winter was coming.

The class was about to end when Lisa told a story: A little apple tree, which stood in a forest of oak trees, prayed to have stars hanging from its branches, as the oak trees appeared to have at night. After months of listening to these prayers, God helped the apple tree to see that it already had stars (the star-shaped pattern of its apple seeds, which is revealed when an apple is cut open horizontally). As I listened to Lisa, my inner child became a little apple tree. It felt so alone in the forest, and it just wanted to be like the oak trees, which represented all the people who had experienced a childhood that did not include torment or terror. My inner child yearned to belong to this lucky group.

While Lisa's voice faded away, silence entered my room, and the story continued its journey inside my soul. I sat in my room with tears in my eyes. I knew that I had many stars that made me special. But sometimes what I saw were the abuse, the violence, the manipulation, the hate, and the conflict of the past, which was where my stars had their origin, I still feared being judged for my past, especially in my professional life as a coach.

I questioned my own value and my own beauty because I knew that my roots were dark and dirty. People might react to these facts with shock and horror. The person I was now was the transformation of the person I had been in the past. And that was my beauty. I had achieved so much in my life. I had set up the life I had always wanted. I had good and trustworthy friends. But I still wanted to be able to tell a different story about my childhood. I did not want to tell people a story about a difficult childhood, with sexual abuse and a father who would not stop sending me unwanted letters. But this was my story. It was the only story I could tell.

The next week, I did my training to become a facilitator of constellations. There were about one hundred people in the room. Half of them were my classmates—some of them therapists or social workers—and the rest were people interested in family constellation therapy, some of whom wanted to be clients and constellate their own stories.

An attractive woman with long brown hair and brown eyes sat on a chair next to the therapist, her head down. The therapist asked her, "What happened in your family?"

The woman replied in a voice that was nearly breaking, "Sexual abuse and violence."

A shocked murmur spread through the room. I saw the stunned faces of my classmates and how some whispered into a neighbor's ear. The client shrank in her seat. She was a picture of me in the past. Looking back, I wasn't sure what had been worse, the actual experiences or other people's reactions, which occurred long after the fact. Seeing the shock and horror in others' eyes had weighed me down. I had experienced only one childhood—I had no other—and I had survived. I didn't know what a happy childhood was. I had nothing with which to compare mine.

Now a classmate-therapist sitting next to me said, "You can never overcome the effects of abuse. Poor thing, she'll have to have therapy for the rest of her life, and she'll never really recover." I would have loved to refute her argument, but in that moment I couldn't find the words to express to her that it is possible to heal abuse, violence, and manipulation. My inability to express my belief left me feeling little and powerless again.

The constellation began and the client chose a representative of the sexual violence and a representative of the other family members. I just sat in my chair and looked at the violence and felt in my body how it had influenced my own life. I looked at it and observed how my body felt. I wanted to integrate it into my life fully, to make the best out of it.

One week later, when I was walking down Portal de Angel, Barcelona's main shopping street, to catch a train to meet a friend, I saw the majestic old buildings and above them the blue sky, which was so much clearer in the winter. I looked up into the sky and tears came to my eyes. I became the little apple tree once again, and I said silently, *I love my stars but I want to be an oak tree. I don't want to be different. I want to be an oak tree. Then I would be truly happy.*

A loving, firm voice answered: *You know that it is not possible.*

I knew that it was not possible, yet I did not want to accept this fact. I saw my father and the heritage of his shadow. I saw the abuse and the horror in other people's eyes. I suddenly felt small and dirty. Why couldn't I be normal, just like everybody else? So I repeated my silent longing: *I feel so little and the oak trees are so tall and majestic. I want to be as tall as the oak trees. Then I would be truly happy.* Tears slowly coursed down my face while I walked down Portal de Angel, holding my silent conversation while I made a slalom to avoid a clash with a group of tourists who did not seem to know what direction they wanted to go. I saw just their fuzzy silhouettes because I was so involved with my inner world.

The response was soft: *But aren't you happy the way you are now?*

I looked around and saw the wonderful blue sky and the warm colors of the houses. I thought about my friends, who helped me so much, and my work. I recognized the richness that I had in my life. I couldn't deny it; I was happy the way I was. So I answered in a small, whispering voice, slightly angry and slightly abashed for being so demanding: *I am happy now. I love my life and I am grateful that I have it. But I want to be able to tell wonderful stories about my family. I do not want to see horror in the eyes of other people. I do not want to be judged.* I still hoped for a confirming answer, for a way to delete my past.

The soft response was, *All you are now has its roots in your childhood, doesn't it? If you are happy now, what is so bad about the past?*

I knew that this was true. Without my story, I'd be a different person. That moment, I looked up at the sky. And I saw so much light, and I knew that I was able to see so much light and beauty in my life because I had experienced darkness, too. Without darkness, there is no light. And if there has been a lot of darkness, there can be a lot of light. I had to accept and surrender. My story was my story, and it was fine as it was. I stopped my inner fight against my story and said simply, *Nothing. Nothing can be so bad about my past. My past was good as it was.* I took a breath. A conflict that had simmered within me for many years was about to go away.

That night when I went to bed, I did not ruminate about the stories of childhood that other people had shared with me. I had my own story. Suddenly, I became aware of the richness of my story: I could discuss healing, accepting, and forgiving. I could talk about finding inner peace, joy, and happiness. And that is what life is all about, isn't it? In the end, what is important is not how you enter the world but how you leave it. That night, I decided that the next time someone said, "A person can never overcome the effects of abuse," I would respond, "I believe that you can. If you want, I can tell you my story."

That day, I decided that I would write down my story to explain to people that it is possible to heal abuse. Before this, I had neither expected to share my story nor seen it as interesting enough or valuable enough to be shared. But now I wanted to speak my truth, to offer a new perspective on society's generic judgment.

I had experienced the burden of being seen as a hopeless case, and it had dragged me down. Now I had proven the contrary: Healing is possible.

Invisible Energies

In my family, spirituality was regarded as silly. There was a strong focus on values, such as family ties, and on possessions, such as a house. With my father, I experienced religion as a means of manipulation. Despite this, I had a strong intuition that I should allow a spiritual reality into my life. First, I had to overcome my doubts.

Spiritual healing was an important step in my own inner process. I started to use Angel cards, just out of curiosity, and followed their guidance. I didn't bother to label who was helping me, such as God or angels. I just accepted that I was being supported by invisible energies. Later, I began to pray again. As a small child I had prayed, but I lost faith after the death of my maternal grandmother when I was ten.

When I was eight, my father forced me to meditate. It was only for a few months, but I hated having to obey his orders and sit in silence.

More than twenty years after my father's meditation experiment, I went into a bookstore in Barcelona. I saw a book with the title *Zen and the Art of Falling in Love* by Brenda Shoshanna. It attracted me, so I bought it and read it. Its contents made me curious, so I started to meditate, first alone and later in a center in Barcelona.

After my first retreat, I decided that I would never, ever serve food during a retreat because I simply believed that I wasn't able to do this. A year later, I participated in another retreat. When I left the dojo (school) after the first meditation in the morning, the following happened: I wanted to have breakfast, which was usually served after the first meditation, so I headed for the line to get my bowl, which was stored outside the dojo.

I wasn't thinking a lot when a nice companion touched my shoulder and asked, "Do you want to do the service?" I froze. A movie started in my inner eye. The monks were sitting in their posture in the dojo by candlelight. They knew the ceremony, with all the precious little gestures, by heart. Their faces serious and deeply focused, they waited for their food. I entered the room with a hot and steaming pot of soup, forgetting all the important details and serving the meal with two left hands, pouring the soup on the floor instead of in the bowl. I saw everyone looking at me with dismay. I had seen others serve the meal in the past, and I had become deeply convinced that I would never be able to serve properly. Then I remembered that things happen when they should happen, so I took a deep breath to collect all my courage and said yes.

I told myself to make the best of it and to serve with love. And that was what I did. At my first service, I crossed in front of the altar to serve on the other side of the room because it was such an invitingly short distance. Some monks tried to signal to me with a smile in their eyes. At first, I did not understand what they wanted to tell me. Then someone told me that it was forbidden. So I took the longer way. I arrived at the next person to be served, and I nearly poured hot water all over him. I grinned. When I looked up, I saw his smiling face. Afterward, I moved more cautiously.

I misunderstood the gesture that indicated that a monk did not want more food. If someone raised a hand, my brain told me to pour more. After a few errors, my brain understood.

Three days later, I passed the Arc de Triomphe on my way home. It was night and the full moon was shining on the monument and the palm trees behind it. I recited, "Om mani padme hum." I really had enjoyed the meditation.

Each meditation retreat helped me explore how I related to other people. It helped me define where I stood in relation to others and to accept that I couldn't control others. It helped me to be authentic when I was with other people and to connect to my inner voice. Meditation is now my daily practice.

Another part of my healing was to forgive. When I was a child, my father's unforgiving attitude always made me feel bad. It didn't feel right, but I grew up in a family where forgiveness didn't exist, so I didn't know how to forgive. But I wanted to forgive my father because I wanted to liberate the resentment I felt toward him, freeing myself of the negative energy. It wasn't about him; it was for my own sake. I read a book titled *La ley del espejo: Una regla mágica que da solución a cualquier problema en la vida* (*The Law of the Mirror: A Magic Rule to Solve Any Problem in Life*) by Yoshinori Noguchi and finally did the exercises in the book during Easter week 2011.

Good Friday was a warm, sunny day that year. I spent it in the darkness of my room, writing down all the negative feelings and emotions I had felt toward my father. I didn't hold back. I connected with my fear, my sadness, and my anger. Sometimes I had to sit down on my bed while tears of frustration streamed down my face. I felt the little child in me who desperately longed for a loving father and never got her wish. I felt the angry child in me who was like a furious red gnome, and I allowed her to express her anger by hitting the pillow while imagining that she was hitting her father. I spent the afternoon jumping from one emotion to another and recording them on paper. That evening, I tore this paper into pieces and burned it to release the negative emotions.

I remembered how I had burned all the letters my father had sent me while I lived in Munich. I had a special box where I kept them, just in case I needed them as proof if I had to go to court. Before I moved to Barcelona, I burned them. I didn't want to take their negative energy with me.

It had been a chilly night in November 2009. I sat on my terrace with a friend, both of us bundled up in winter clothing. In front of us stood the barbecue grill. Next to my chair was a huge pile of letters and books my father had sent me. They were full of blame, judgment, and accusations directed at my mother, her family, and me. I didn't know who behaved more badly in the marriage, my father or my mother. Each did harm in his or her own way and each made mistakes. I couldn't judge. In the end, both had been responsible for the failure of their marriage.

Piece by piece, I threw the papers into the flames. The flames burned high in the air. I got a bucket of water to ensure that my terrace would not catch fire. It took us several hours to burn everything.

Now I watched the paper with my negative emotions recorded on it. It was burning in the flames of a barbecue, and I felt calm, just like a lake without ripples.

The following day, I did the next step. I sat down on my sofa and searched for my father's motives for his behavior. I saw him as an adolescent who found his father at home, dead by his own hand. I imagined the immense pain he must have felt in the moment. I saw an even younger child living through World War II in Germany. What was it like to be one-half Croatian and live in a Germany that discriminated against non-Germans? To live in constant fear that he might be put into a concentration camp? I imagined his fears and insecurities. At his age, he was not able to deal with the pain or the situation. So he shut down his feelings. In my father's generation, one did not consult a therapist, so he closed off the option of seeking professional help. He was a hurt adult who committed cruel acts. I was able to see that he had done what he had done because he had not wanted to feel his pain. He had done the best he could, and now he had to live with the consequences of his actions. I was responsible for my own healing; I could not fix him.

Then I wrote down everything I was thankful for. I saw

myself as a six-year-old again, sitting at his breakfast table and enjoying bread that was spread thickly with strawberry jam. I remembered his *eierbrote* and how much I had enjoyed eating it with ketchup. I remembered that I sat at his kitchen table and watched him preparing his special potato salad, Bavarian style, which I liked very much. Then I saw myself in his new red sports car, sitting in the back and singing wholeheartedly, "My Bonnie Lies Over the Ocean." While singing it, I always felt that something special would happen. (While writing down this experience, I started to smile. When I started therapy three years ago, my therapist asked me what good things had happened with my father. I went home and sat down at the kitchen table and desperately tried to remember the good things. I couldn't remember anything. I judged myself: *It can't be like that; there must have been something good.* But I couldn't remember. Now I am able to recall the good memories; doing so takes a load off my mind.)

Then it was time to use the power of intention and words, so I made this declaration: "For my own happiness, calmness, and freedom, I forgive my father." I stood in front of my altar and said those magical words. Then for thirty minutes I repeated, "I forgive my father." While I did so, emotions came up again. I just allowed them to be. I repeated my intention: "For my own happiness, calmness, and freedom, I forgive my father." I was forgiving my father for my own sake.

Then I wrote down everything that I felt sorry for. How I broke off contact in a way that wasn't right. I hadn't stated my reasons. I hadn't spoken my truth when I was with him. I also wrote, "I feel sorry that I don't want to have contact with you."

The next step was something I had learned from him: I wrote down my definition of a good father. I also recorded my ideas of what a child needs. I transformed the negative experiences into positive acts.

Finally, I declared, "I forgive you." The next week, I spent five minutes each day imagining my father in my mind's eye and telling him, "Thank you, Papa." I thanked him for my life, for my Croatian roots, and for the person I am.

Over the next few months, my inner peace about my father grew. My work regarding him continued during a coaching session a few weeks later. My coach was on a business trip in Malaysia, and we were typing messages into Skype. Suddenly, I received a message: "I know that this question is not in the scope of your goal, but what would you need to change *within yourself* so that you could have contact with your father?"

The words hit me in the face like an iron fist. One part of me became angry. I didn't want to have contact with him. My father would need to change, not me. I wrote back, "What do I have to change? I did not manipulate. I was a child." *Why does he ask me this?* I was angry.

The response came quickly: "I understand. Yet think about the answer: What would you need to change *within yourself* so that you could have contact with your father?"

I looked at the screen. I had no idea what to do. I had tried for so many years to have a relationship with him. It had been a relief when I cut off contact with him. So I replied, "I don't want to have contact with him. I don't have an answer."

Yet the question lingered in my mind; the wheels in my head were spinning. What did I still have to learn? The next morning, I was still furious. I wrote to my coach: "For so many years, I have tried to overcome the effects of abuse, manipulation, and violence. For so many years, I have been aware that I might become an abusive person myself because I was a victim. The abuse is a dark shadow in my life. You wrote that you understood. I want to ask you, do you really understand what it means to have survived sexual abuse and violence? Do you really understand what it means to be aware that you could become an abuser if you don't take responsibility for healing yourself? Do you really understand how I feel?"

It was the first time that I had shared with another person my pain and my desperation about the possibility of becoming an abuser. So far, this possibility had stayed in the back of my mind; I had never dared to share it. My responsibility to ensure that it would never happen weighed heavily on me. Teary-eyed, I sat on my sofa. I imagined myself with a loving partner and children. Instead, I sat alone on my sofa, fighting with the shadows of my past in order to heal myself. I felt lonely and isolated.

I sat there and breathed deeply. I wasn't angry about the question. I was angry that I didn't know the answer. I silently sent the question to the Universe: *Please help me. What do I have to change within myself so that I can have contact with my father?*

The answer came suddenly during the day: *You need to increase your inner peace and trust in yourself.*

I smiled. I had found the answer I needed. I would not be able to control what my father did. I could only take care of myself. I meditated to connect with my inner peace.

Some days later, my coach answered me: "You know that things you look at lose their control over you." He was right. I had looked at my past. I wouldn't repeat my father's destiny.

Six weeks later, I launched my website for my business. From then on, I would be visible to the public. I was thirty-seven years old, and I had stopped trying to hide from my father. He couldn't control my life any longer. I would continue my journey in plain sight.

Another part of my healing was visualizations. One visualization changed my life. It was a Saturday evening, and we had class all day. It was already dark outside. Twenty people were sitting in a circle, and our trainer asked us to close our eyes and breathe deeply. I closed my eyes and breathed. I heard his voice as it guided me tenderly: "Imagine that it is your birthday, and you want to throw a birthday party. You prepare everything. You look for the perfect location."

I saw a wonderful beach somewhere in Asia. There was an open area with four wooden pillars, which were covered by a ceiling made from colorful cloths. From the ceiling hung some pink shawls that danced in the soft breeze.

"You make a list of your invitees: your friends, your family, your partner."

I wrote a long list of people and hoped that they all would catch a plane to visit me.

"Now the day of the party has come. You are at the location. You see the first guest arriving."

I stood on this wonderful beach. It was dark and the sea was moving softly. I was surrounded by the colorful shawls. I wore a halter dress. I looked beautiful. Music was playing quietly. My first friends arrived. I hugged them and we started to dance and have fun.

"Now more people arrive. You greet them."

I saw two people in the distance, a man and a woman. They approached. They talked to each other in a friendly way. They smiled at each other. The woman touched the arm of the man. I recognized them: my parents! I could hardly believe it. They hugged me. My father stood in front of me, looked deeply into my eyes, and said, "I am proud of you." I stood there. I still could hardly believe it had happened. I saw my parents dancing together, not as a couple but as friends. I observed them and smiled.

"Slowly, open your eyes again, and come back to the present moment."

I opened my eyes. My world had changed. I had seen my parents together, having a good time. I had talked to my father, just as in any normal family. I saw this as a sign that I had healed my past, and that gave me confidence and security.

A further step in my healing was the training Spiritual Opening for Healing, which allowed me to connect with invisible energies, both for my own healing and to facilitate my clients' healing. It was led by Margarita, a woman who radiated unconditional love; she became my *maestra* (spiritual master teacher) and a dear friend. I met her for the first time when I did a constellation to heal my relationship with my father. It was the first time in my life that I could talk about the sexual violence while feeling inner peace. I was thirty-eight years old.

During the training, Margarita proposed a shamanic ritual. Shamans believe that part of the soul can be lost due to trauma. This lost part of the soul will need to be reclaimed. For many years, I had felt as if I did not possess a soul. At this point, I had reconnected with my soul, but I still felt that something was missing. My soul felt incomplete. So her words made perfect sense to me. Margarita instructed the other participants to make a circle with their chairs; she told me to sit in the middle of the circle. Following Margarita's guidance, I closed my eyes and connected with myself as a three-year-old who was being sexually assaulted. Then I said in a loud voice, "Soul, come back to me!" I visualized the part that I had lost during the abuse as a light coming toward me from a distance and entering my chest. Tears ran down my face as the other participants embraced me. I was immeasurably grateful that I had recovered something precious that I had once believed was impossible to recover.

Rituals enriched my life. I lit a candle on the birthdays of my late mother and my late grandmother. I went into a Barcelona church, Santa Maria del Mar, to light a candle for my family, and I imagined my father and my mother standing behind me and giving me strength. I took a bath with roses to heal past relationships.

I learned and practiced different techniques of spiritual healing, connecting with my higher self and with universal energy. A friend helped me heal my body energetically. My body still reacted with fear to men. I had transformed this fear on an emotional level and on a mental level, yet it still was in my body. With the help of my friend, I was able to transform this. At the age of thirty-eight, I was at last able to make love with a man without fear in my body; I opened up and let go.

Over the years, I experienced significant inner changes, yet some doubts about the existence of this invisible support remained. I asked the Universe for a sign. Two weeks later—December 16, 2012, the birthday of my wonderful late maternal grandmother—I went into the Parc de la Ciutadella in Barcelona, where I fed a colony of abandoned and feral cats with another woman, Vicki, each Sunday. It was nearly dark.

Suddenly, a man, a shipbuilder from Port Olimpic, arrived with a box. Vicki, a small, energetic lady in her sixties who had fed the cats in the park for more than twenty years, looked into it and screamed, "Look at this!"

I saw a little kitten, just a few weeks old, with his two back paws taped with bandages.

While she tried to give him some pills to decrease his pain, she whispered to me, "He won't survive the night out here in the colony. His eyes are cloudy and his tongue is already white."

Tearfully, I touched the little head. His eyes looked at me, full of pain. His fur felt stiff. "Can we do anything? I could catch a taxi and take him to a clinic." Vicki nodded and called the organization responsible for the colony. They said yes, take him to a clinic.

Vicki and I left the park with the box. While we walked, the kitten was jostled and he let out a scream of pain in a thin voice. On the sidewalk, Vicki put down the box and tried to move him into a better position. A taxi stopped and I got inside, carrying the box. While the driver searched for directions on the route planner, Vicki said, "They'll have to amputate the leg."

I nodded. "If the little one survives, he can live with me." Twenty minutes later, I arrived at the veterinarian's office. I took the box into the emergency room, and the doctor lifted the kitten out of the box. I left the room when they removed the bandages. I couldn't look at the blood. Twenty minutes later, I was waiting on a plastic chair in the hallway when the doctor came out, his face worried.

"We have to amputate at least one leg."

I asked cautiously, "Will he survive the night?"

They would try to stabilize him. I left the clinic. The doctors would do what they could for his tiny, battered body.

I went home and gave the kitten a name: Angel. Then I started to pray to the Universe, did my rituals for spiritual healing, and sent Reiki, a type of energetic healing, to Angel. After three days, I received the first information. The list of problems was seemingly overwhelming.

The first day, he had a cardiac arrest and they resuscitated him. Then he needed a blood transfusion. He was nearly starved and had necrosis in his two back legs. He must have been lying injured at the harbor for several days. The third day, the little cat started to eat. The veterinarian said, "It is very likely that he will lose both back legs and stay a bit stupid because of the cardiac arrest. Anyway, if this cat survives, I will believe in God." He put his chance of survival at 5 percent.

On Christmas Eve, I was allowed to visit him for the first time. I sat in the animal clinic with a bundle of towels on my knees, and in the middle of the bundle there was little Angel. I returned every second day.

One week later, on New Year's Eve, another veterinarian told me, "This cat will not survive. He has too many injuries." I looked at her and asked silently, *But he has survived for two weeks, hasn't he? He eats, doesn't he? Why are you seeing it as so dark?* I did not dare to discuss Angel with her. I left in tears because of the apparent hopelessness of the situation. But on my way home, I bought a candle as a sign of my trust that he would survive. The candle burned each day. I continued with my visits and with the Reiki. A friend of mine sent Reiki, too.

Two weeks later, they amputated the first leg. That day, I asked my own cats' veterinarian how to handle a cat that was missing both back legs.

He looked at me, worried, and said, "That will not work."

I left the animal clinic and decided to trust.

One week later, they amputated the second leg. Then they gave me hope for the first time: "If everything goes fine, we will dismiss him next week." A week later, the veterinarian told me, "You can take him home on Friday. That's a miracle."

Two months after I had taken him to the clinic, I was allowed to take my little cat home. The veterinarian gave me diapers. He believed that Angel wouldn't be able to use the cat box properly because of the missing legs. I decided that he'd learn. He learned within two days.

Angel fought for his life and never gave up. He suffered a lot in the first months of his life, and I wanted him to enjoy the rest of it. I trusted that he could do everything that he wanted. He surprised me every day. I was terribly proud of him when I saw him for the first time in the cave of the cat tree, which is 8 inches above the floor. He loves to play soccer with a little ball and scoots around the apartment with surprising speed. Much of the day, he sleeps peacefully with Loki and Thor on my bed. In the beginning, Loki and Thor seemed to be afraid of Angel because he moved so strangely. I think that they could not even make out whether he was a cat. But after some months of confusion, they adjusted and now live together peacefully.

I believe that it was a miracle that Angel survived. I believe that invisible energies exist and that they support us. Call it energy, call it the Universe, call it God, or maybe call it angels. It doesn't matter. My life changed in a miraculous way the moment that I asked for invisible support and allowed that help to happen. I know that these energies helped me to heal and helped me to realize changes that I never would have believed possible. So I pray, meditate, sing mantras, visualize, or do spiritual rituals daily. I choose what feels right for me. My practice helps me connect with my inner voice, my own resources. It brings me inner peace and points out the best path for me.

Integrating Two Worlds

Through my own healing, I was able to integrate the two worlds of my father and my mother with each other and with my own world. It was a slow process and it started with accepting my father as he is. The more I healed my relationship with my father, the better I was able to accept myself, let go of his rejection of me, and decide for myself what I wanted. Finally, I decided that I would pursue a career similar to his. He was a trainer; I became a coach and a trainer. Ten years earlier, I never would have believed this was possible.

For many years, I didn't know what to do with my Croatian roots. My father rejected his Croatian roots. When I was seven, I was angry with him because he did not speak Croatian. I wanted to be bilingual. When I was twenty-six, I hated my Croatian last name and rejected this part of my roots, as my father did. Sometimes people said to me, "You speak German well for a foreigner." I never knew what to respond. I was German, yet I never really felt at home in Germany.

Over the years, I became curious about Croatia, especially after I moved to Spain. Then, during a constellation in 2012, a representative for Croatia entered the constellation, and in the same moment, I had to cry. There was a deep yearning in my soul to connect with this country. I decided to visit Croatia. I wasn't sure where my ancestors came from, so I planned a trip to Zagreb with my friend Sabine to connect with the spirits of my ancestors.

My trip started on Good Friday at 4:00 a.m. I caught a taxi at

Via Laietana, which was nearly empty at that time—just a few drunken people coming home from a party—to go to the airport. My first stop was Munich, where I had a layover of several hours. Sabine had a later flight; we would meet in Zagreb.

I used this time to visit my sister and to have brunch with her. We sat together at a round table in a café I had visited while I lived in Munich and had lattes with *brez'n* (crusty Bavarian pretzels) and German buns.

Then I got on the small propeller aircraft that would take me to Zagreb. When I arrived, I saw many green bushes and the temperature was a bit warmer than in Munich. I caught a bus to the hotel and listened to the people speaking. I didn't catch the meaning, yet sometimes I had the impression that I heard some Spanish words.

After I had left my bags in the hotel, I started to stroll through the city. I didn't plan where to go to, just followed my inner voice as I meandered through the streets of the city.

I crossed a square, Zrinjevac, which was bordered by majestic plane trees that did not yet have leaves. Zrinjevac had colorful flowerbeds, ornate fountains, and a music pavilion. I sat down on a bench for a moment and enjoyed the peacefulness. In my inner eye, I saw my ancestors wandering around in the park on a warm day in spring, enjoying the songs of the birds. When I continued walking, I found a street with small cafés where people sat outside. I saw people greeting their friends with a hug or just sitting and having coffee while reading a newspaper. It was a friendly and joyful atmosphere. In the distance, I saw a huge cathedral on a small hill; the large building towered above the houses. Sabine arrived late that night, when I was already in my hotel room.

The next day, we hiked up the hill to the cathedral. We went inside and I lit a candle for my ancestors. I closed my eyes and said silently, *I respect you. I need you. I came to your country, which I consider my country, to recover my roots. Your earth is my earth. Please help me with this.* I stood there for a while before I left.

We continued exploring the city, including the botanical garden. Finally, we returned to Zrinjevac, the square where I had visited the first day. There, I made another ritual to connect with my ancestors. I felt that it was the right place for this.

Sabine waited on a bench while I went to a fountain. I stood in front of the fountain, closed my eyes, and visualized that roots grew out of my feet and extended down into the earth. I imagined that they would extend over all Croatia. Then I said to the country, *Please help me find peace, serenity, balance, and tranquility. Help me to rebirth in my land, so that I am complete.*

When I was finished, my body asked me to make the sign of the cross. I had never done this before, as I did not connect with the Catholic religion. I asked Sabine and she showed me how to do it correctly.

On Sunday, we returned to Munich, Sabine said good-bye, and I met my sister at the airport to have dinner.

Late at night, I arrived at Barcelona Airport again. I caught a cab and the driver asked me where I had been. "Croatia," I said.

When we arrived at Via Laietana again, he got out of the cab to retrieve my suitcase from the trunk. Putting it on the ground, he said, "Now you have arrived on terra firma." His comment made me smile.

The trip gave Croatia a good place in my heart. After that trip, I noticed that I was able to look at Germany and at Croatia and integrate both countries into my mental life and my emotional life. I felt at home and I felt that I was in the right place. I lived as a foreigner in a foreign country, able to see two other countries peacefully.

Finally, my father.

His first card arrived in Barcelona. I sent him another letter telling him that I didn't want contact with him. Some weeks later, the next card arrived. Its front was a photo of the Nymphenburg Palace park. It showed a majestic tree in autumn; its leaves had already disappeared. In the background was Lake Badenburg, the bigger lake in the park, and at the far shore of the lake was the elegant, small, round white temple of Apollo, which was built in the shape of a monopteros (a structure with no walls but with a circular colonnade that supports a roof). I had drawn it once when I took a drawing class in the park. I turned the card around and read the following:

"Some people say that you cheated us, dear Nana, because you let us support you for years and pretended that you were part of the family. But we see it in a different way. We were happy to help our young daughter. We like to bear you in mind. And you are right: The past is gone. But at the same time, the past continues living in you. Why speak badly about the good that was? We have behaved fairly. How about some respect from your side?"

I read these words again: "the past continues living in you."

Once, I would have interpreted the phrase as a threat. I would have feared how my father's words might affect me. Now I responded to my father silently: "Yes, the past continues living in me but not in a way that you can imagine."

Two days later, I participated in my training for family constellations. This month, the topic was families, and the title was Where Life Can Grow. We were in our final round, saying what had moved us that weekend. It was a large circle, about twenty people, some of whom I knew well, others not at all. About fifteen people took a turn; many of them said that they were grateful for their children. Then it was my turn.

What should I say? I could say something light and breezy. Or I could show up and be honest. I stood up for my truth, which most of my classmates were not familiar with, and said, "I thought a lot about family and what the word means to me. My original family taught me a lot and was connected with a lot of pain. My father has sent me letters I do not want all my adult life, even though I have said several times that I do not want to have contact with him. He has never stopped. In Germany, I had a secret address. Now he has found me in Barcelona." My inner child felt shame.

My classmates said compassionately, "Breathe. Just breathe."

I smiled. How well I knew to do this, and how difficult it was sometimes. So I said, "Yes, I just need a bit of time because inside me is an inner child who feels a lot of shame right now." Slowly, I started to breathe again. Then I said, "I am really grateful that there are also families of souls and families of animals, because without them I would not have survived." Again, I had to concentrate on breathing. It took me some time to get my sentences out. After a while, I looked up into the circle of my classmates. I saw compassion in their eyes, not judgment.

My teacher sat next to me, and she said with joy in her voice, "Well, when my inner child heard that her inner child felt shame, she just wanted to grab her and go out and play a bit."

I had to laugh.

Sharing the reality I lived in and sharing the experiences I had helped me to liberate my past. After many years, the shadow of my father has faded away because I was able to share my truth and I was true to myself. That was what gave me inner peace.

The invisible life-fight between him and me is finished. He has his life and I have mine. He was my greatest teacher, spurring me to find myself, accept myself, and learn what true love is. He motivated me to make the best out of my life and to live life to the fullest. For this, I am grateful.

One month later, I was in another training, Stories and Metaphors. It was the final exercise. We pinned papers on each other's backs, and everybody took turns writing what they appreciated about the others. When the exercise was over, my neighbor unpinned my paper for me, and I read the comments. Somebody had written that I combined vulnerability and force. When I read it, I had to smile. Finally, I really had united the two main traits of my parents. I had been able to unite within me the two worlds that constantly had been at war. My inner conflict was gone.

During my childhood, my mother told one story, my father another. The two stories collided with each other just like two magnets, each with its own North pole. I could not make sense of this. For many years, I closed my eyes, unable to look at their stories. It was as if the two contradictory realities had stolen my voice, my identity.

I set sail in a boat whose sail had been torn from the mast, a boat exposed to the winds without any chance to influence its own direction. In the beginning, I was nailed to the deck, trying to get up but failing. Then I got up and fought with invisible enemies. My anger gave me the energy to look for better solutions. Later, I connected with my wise part, which had always accompanied me invisibly even though I hadn't been aware of it. I allowed it to guide me and trusted it. This way, the sail became reconnected to the mast, and I became the captain of the boat. It did not matter where the wind came from, I decided my course and steered the boat in the direction I wanted it to go.

My story integrated the forces that lived within me in a way that can nurture me. Now the conflicting stories of my parents are at rest, their battle ended.

A Relationship
Is a Dance of Two

It took me more than two years after Sam to start dating again. They were all occasions that developed naturally because I never used dating websites. Also, it took me months to find out whether I was interested in a man, so it didn't happen very often.

The first date I went on was with a colleague. It was our only date, because I found out he had a wife and child. That moment, I lost interest.

Some months later, I had to contact another coach, Sergio, who lived in Madrid. We knew each other only by telephone, yet I felt that he was interested in me. We had similar interests and he had some interesting projects, so before I went to Madrid for a training, I dropped him a line.

He responded immediately: "Great, we can meet here in Madrid. When do you arrive? I can pick you up at the train station." I decided to go at my own pace and replied that he did not need to pick me up; we could meet on Friday after the training. Two days later, I left for Madrid. I would meet a man for dinner whom I had not seen before—a new experience for me. I arrived on Thursday, and on Friday I searched for the building where the Relationship Training course would take place. It was a chilly day in April, and I was impressed with and intimidated by Madrid's elegance and grandeur. While Barcelona had buildings with a dreamy, sometimes shabby, charm, the buildings in

Madrid were majestic, and the women and men were elegant in their suits.

Finally, I reached the building, which was close to the famous Prado Museum. I went up the staircase and entered the lobby. I saw about eight people I did not know. Suddenly, I saw someone I did know—Alicia, a classmate from the first three modules, which I had done in Barcelona. I felt relieved. She approached me, gave me a hug, and said, "Great to see you here in Madrid!" Then she introduced me to her classmates. Later, I sat in the training room. It had snow-white walls with some ornaments on them and a wooden floor. The sun shone through the huge windows.

We would each have a partner and work on an exercise together. I decided to work on my nervousness about the date. My classmate, a blonde woman, asked me, "So what is your highest dream about your date with this man? What would be the best possible outcome?"

I looked at her and said, "Well, if it works out perfectly—if I fall in love with him and he falls in love with me—we could have a relationship." I smiled.

"What would be the worst possible outcome for this date?"

She looked in my eyes and I said, "I fall in love with him but he is not interested. But I have dealt with this situation before. I might feel bad for a few days, and then it will be over. In the end, I can only win. I go there and be who I am. So there is not really a problem. What ever happens, I am safe." I looked at her and felt how my eyes started to sparkle. My body became light. There was really nothing bad that could happen. I could only win and maybe I would get to know an interesting man.

Later, at 6:00 p.m., I walked down the street to Starbucks. Suddenly, Madrid seemed a much better place. Through the window of Starbucks, I saw a man. He had dark blond hair, and he was tall and good looking. I knew that it was Sergio. He came out of Starbucks and asked me whether I was Natalie. We hugged. Then we went for a walk trough Retiro Park, and later we caught a taxi to have tea in a wonderful tearoom with a Chinese flair. Then he invited me for dinner. The next day, we met again.

Some weeks later, he asked me whether I'd like to go to a meditation weekend with him. I emailed him yes and asked for more details. No answer. After a week, I felt strange about this and sent him another email asking about his plans.

The next day, I started working at my desk in an especially good mood because I had woken up with a German song humming in my head, "Wunder Geschehen" ("Miracles Happen"). I remembered that I had once read that a healed inner child has a sense of miracles. I had never felt it before, but now I knew that miracles could happen. I saw it as a sign that my inner child felt well. Sitting in front of my Mac, I listened to a song on YouTube and started singing it, my favorite blue and white coffeepot at my side. It was a huge pot and very special for me because it was a present from my sister. Somehow, I made a stupid movement, and the coffeepot fell to the floor. The song played in the background while tears came to my eyes. A German saying came to mind: A broken fragment brings good luck. I took a breath and thought that this all might be a signal that something good would happen.

I looked in my inbox and saw a message from Sergio. I opened it and read, "I do not know yet whether I will go to the retreat. And anyway, the distance from Madrid to Barcelona . . . " I understood. He was not as interested as much as I had hoped.

So I replied, "Well, for me it is now time to let it go. I wish you good luck." I did not want to waste my time with somebody who was not interested. If a man has doubts, I can't do anything to convince him to stay with me. I smiled. I noticed that I had more self-esteem when I listened to my inner voice.

Later, I met Jaime in my dojo. He was tall, with blond hair and impressive blue eyes. We talked a lot about personal development and our dreams. We knew each other for five months before we had our first date. A few weeks later, he called to tell me that I was exactly the kind of independent woman he sought for a relationship; at that stage, I saw him as a good partner. We made plans for our future, we went dancing, we went to a meditation retreat in France, and we went hiking. I got to know his friends. It seemed to be going in a good direction during the first three months, so much so that we started to talk about moving in together.

In September, I attended the wedding of a friend in Vigo in northwest Spain. At the party, I shared about my new relationship: "We met in our dojo. We had a few dates, and three months ago, he called me and said, 'Natalie, I was just riding my moped and I knew it. You are the woman I want to spend my life with. I have always looked for an independent woman like you. You are exactly the woman I need. Do you want to have a relationship with me?' We have so much in common. He likes the same things that I do, and he wants to support me with my business. Actually, we plan to move in together." I felt how my eyes brightened while I told my story. I had really made it. This time, I had managed to kiss him when I felt it appropriate. I had allowed myself the time I needed before I had sex with him. I was healed.

A friend asked, "So if I write down what I want, I'll attract it?"

"Sure, you need to focus on what you want and be clear about it."

He was slightly skeptical. "And what if it does not work out?"

I laughed. "Well, then you let go of the relationship and think about what you have to learn. Maybe you need to adjust your love card. I needed all of my past relationships to define what I really wanted in a relationship. Even though it was painful that they did not work out, they helped me to figure out what I really wanted and needed."

He smiled. "I'll give it a try."

I returned on Sunday. From the airport in Vigo, I called Vicki and told her that I wouldn't be feeding the cat colony that week.

I wanted to spend Sunday evening with Jaime. Later, I arrived at Barcelona Airport. It had been four years since I was picked up by my partner at an airport. I went through the automatic frosted glass doors of the arrivals hall and looked for Jaime. I saw him standing in the back. Smiling, I walked in his direction. I looked at him. Somehow, he seemed different, just like a strict father. I ignored my impression and gave him a kiss. He hardly reacted. I was a bit irritated but didn't think anything bad. We went to his car.

Suddenly, he said, "That is not OK." His voice was full of anger. "What is not OK?"

"You have to tell me that you missed me. When you have been gone for the weekend, you have to tell me that you missed me."

I did not know what to say. I had thought about him in Vigo—thought about what I liked about him—yet I had not missed him. I missed very few people. So I just answered honestly: "Well, I thought about you. But I normally don't miss a person if I do not see him for just two nights. It was just two nights."

He grunted. Without a word, he stalked off to his car, with me following. I had visualized our reception differently. I felt confused. We sat together in the car to drive to the beach. He continued complaining: "I don't like it when you call me *guapo*. It does not sound loving. You need to express your love to me in a better way!"

I listened to his words, a bit hurt. For me, it was really special to call him *guapo*, or handsome one. But I said, "For me, it means something special. But if you do not like it, I'll change it."

He was dissatisfied with my reply. For the next ten minutes, he continued pointing out what I had to change. I felt smaller and smaller. I hardly knew how I could fulfill all his needs. It seemed that I had done everything wrong. When we arrived at the beach, I broke into tears, feeling completely helpless and confused. The relationship was going in the wrong direction.

Four days later, he sat down on the thick carpet in his meditation room. I looked at him briefly. I was working on my computer. For a moment, I asked myself why he had to be in the room where I was working. In four days, I had acquired the impression that he always sat by my side, even though his apartment had four rooms. No matter where I was, he sat down next to me.

Our discussions had continued every day. He always had a need to discuss something. I longed for a few minutes of privacy to send information to a client, but I said nothing. I could perceive his anger. He seemed to be boiling over like hot milk that rose in the pot. I had the impression that he would interrupt me. Some minutes later, Jaime said, "This cannot be like this. You have to smile when I am around, and you have to kiss me when I come home." I looked up, slightly reluctant, and responded that I had said hello, that we had talked briefly, and that I needed 40 minutes alone to finish my work. He looked at me harshly. His face was hard and strict like a draconian father.

Silently, I asked myself whether he really was the man I had gotten to know a few months earlier, the one who had told me that he wanted a relationship with an independent woman. The day before, he had had a nervous attack because he believed that I was deeply influenced by my family and that he would suffer the consequences. I had been irritated by his words and wondered how he could think that, given that he knew my personal story. I hadn't met many people who had worked so much with their family story. I had started to defend myself, but then I got angry because the discussion definitely violated my boundaries.

I said, "You know, if you think that I am deeply influenced by my family and that it will be bad for you, that is your opinion. I know that my family does not have a bad influence over me. It does not make sense to continue this discussion." I got up and went to the balcony to have some privacy. There, I cried because I felt verbally attacked—a red flag.

Later that night, he came to me and asked, "Do you want something to eat?"

The only thing I really needed was my privacy and to finish my work, so I said no.

Ten minutes later, he came into the room and put a plate with cheese and grapes on the table. I noticed that he ignored my words, and I knew that some nice gestures are not nice but part of the poisonous game of manipulation—another red flag.

Now, sitting on the floor, he said, "No, no, this cannot be. If it continues like this for another six months, you will damage me."

Damage him? Had he really said that I would damage him? What must he be thinking about me if he believed that I wanted to damage him?

He continued in a sweet voice: "You only have to change your behavior, not your essence. I really like your essence. You have changed so much in your life—it is easy for you to change your behavior." That was the third red flag. My inner voice told me that it was time to go.

I asked him calmly, "Do you really think you are being kind to yourself to stay with a person who will damage you?"

He did not even get my question. He continued to explain to me what I had to change. The situation was not at all loving for me. The past week had been horrible for me. I didn't want to continue fighting with him any longer. The kindest thing was to let him go.

"Jaime, it is time to stop our relationship now. It does not make any sense for me to continue like this." He did not listen and continued talking, trapped in his anger. While listening to him, I wrote a message to my landlord to ask him whether I could stay in my apartment. I had canceled my lease only the day before due to our plans to live together. Now I wanted to recall the cancellation of my lease. After half an hour listening to Jaime's words, I repeated calmly, "Jaime, you do not need to discuss this with me. The relationship is over."

He did not seem to understand. I left the room and he followed me and said, "A relationship is about discussing problems. We will discuss problems all the time. A relationship is a struggle." I thought, *No, that is not my opinion.* Aloud, I said, "For me, a relationship is about sharing love and inspiring the other person and feeling joy." Then I added what I should have said to Paolo: "If I listen to your words, you want this kind of woman." I made a huge step to my left side and continued: "But even though you say you want an independent woman, you don't. You want a woman who is right next to you all the time." I moved close to him. Then I stepped back to the spot far away from him and said, "I am this woman and I do not want to change who I am."

Ten minutes later, I left his apartment.

Jaime continued to follow me. He always found a charming reason to do so. He sent a large bouquet of flowers to me at a training. I told him to leave me alone and that I didn't want his flowers; I gave them to a friend. Then he visited me on a Sunday at the colony of abandoned and feral cats to ask me for a second chance. He promised that he would change. I said no. Then I found him in front of my house when I took out the garbage. He told me that he had had an intuition that I wanted to go to the movies with him. I told him no. That evening, I sent him an email to tell him that I didn't want any contact with him. When Vicki told me that he had looked for me at the colony of abandoned and feral cats while I was away in London, I asked a lawyer friend to call him and tell him to stay away from me. She did and he never contacted me again.

Jaime showed the typical pattern of a manipulative man. When I first got to know him, he was nice and charming. Once he thought that he possessed me, he changed his face and started his manipulations. I was able to see his manipulations and get out of the vicious cycle within a few days. I was angry with myself for some weeks because I had been attracted to him, but in the beginning I couldn't see his true face: he was showing me a false face. In this relationship, I listened to my inner voice. I had learned how to protect myself and how to ask for help. I believe that I needed Jaime to show me that I would clearly say no to any manipulative man. In the end, I was proud of myself.

And then there was Ben, my former manager. I had known him for fourteen years. He had always been special to me. Fourteen years earlier, he was the only man with whom I could share an office and not feel fear. He was the only manager who could motivate me and manage my strong desire to grow. I had always felt respected by him and I had never, ever had a better manager. He lived with his partner and his four children in Denver. He was one of the very few men I had trusted from the start. During the preceding three years, he had phoned me every few months, and we had talked about relationships. Once in a while, I missed him a bit and I dreamed about seeing him again.

It was a warm evening in October 2012 when I sat down at my computer to work. The window to my balcony was open, and the voices of people speaking on the road below filled my apartment. Suddenly, a Skype message appeared: "Are you there?" It was Ben.

"Sure. How are you?"

He phoned me and we started talking. I told him the story about Jaime and he said, "The guy from the meditation center you mentioned when we spoke in May? I knew from the beginning that he wasn't the right man for you." I smiled internally. After each failed relationship attempt, he had said the same thing: "He wasn't the right man for you." Today I exclaimed, slightly frustrated, "Well, I just want to find a normal man and have a healthy relationship. What is so complicated about that?"

He answered quietly, "I consider myself to be normal, but I am still in a relationship." Suddenly, there was a subtle energy shift, and something deep inside my heart stirred. I suddenly saw him with new eyes. For a moment, I caught myself thinking that Ben would be the right man for me: we had so much in common. I rejected this thought immediately. He had a partner. He had kids. After we hung up, I sat in my apartment, confused. What had happened? What did Ben mean to me? I sent him a message, more to confirm his status than to say anything.

"Thank you for your friendship and your relationship advice. The next time, I will call you before I start something new."

A few hours later, he answered: "As you know, I like you very much. You are attractive, intelligent, and witty. For a woman like you, the right man exists. I hope that you find a man who loves and respects you as you are."

Tears pricked my eyelids. I had just become aware how much Ben meant to me. I hadn't seen it before or I hadn't allowed myself to see it because he was in a relationship. This was an impossible story. I decided to withdraw and to forget about him. As the weeks passed, I walked through the streets of Barcelona and couldn't get the song "My Bonnie Lies Over the Ocean" out of my head. It came up in my mind again and again. I did not want to feel anything for a man in a relationship. I did not want to feel anything for a man who was unavailable.

In the preceding three years, I had watched *When Harry Met Sally* about thirty times. Why did I love this movie so much? I didn't know. Suddenly, my fondness for this movie made perfect sense. Sally fell in love with her friend. I felt that I was about to fall in love with Ben, even though he was far away. Immediately, I asked myself whether I was interested in him only because he was unavailable. *No, it doesn't feel like that.* But it didn't matter what I felt; I didn't contact him because he had a relationship.

Five months later, I saw another Skype message from Ben: "Are you there? How are you?"

This time, I didn't know what to do. Reluctantly, I answered him after a few days: "I'm great! I'm forty now! How are you?"

He answered, "I'm single again. It's a bit strange. I'm glad you're doing well. I had the suspicion that you had a new partner because I hadn't heard from you for so long."

He is single again. I had never expected that to happen. I was sorry about his broken relationship while my heart jumped for joy. I wrote, "I am sorry to hear that. Near or far, no man in my life." *But a man in Denver means a lot to me.*

Some weeks later, I confessed to a friend in Munich that I felt something for Ben. She knew both of us, and her reaction astonished me: "I'm not surprised. I have always noticed that he means a lot to you. Sometimes I thought that the two of you would make a good couple."

After this, Ben and I started to communicate regularly. I knew that I had to see him again to know what I really felt for him. So I took a risk and invited him to visit me in Barcelona.

He answered, "I was really thinking about going to Europe in May. I'd like to see Barcelona, but only if it wouldn't bother you."

I panicked. What if he didn't like me at all? What if I fell in love? I examined all the possible what-if scenarios. But without seeing him, I would not find out what would happen, so I replied that it wouldn't bother me.

Our contact continued and we exchanged photos. Ben started to call me honey in his emails. Once, he wrote that he had always had felt a special emotional connection with me. Another time, he wrote that he had dreamed that we were lying together on the beach, holding hands. Then he wrote that he couldn't wait to see me again. The defenses that I had built around my heart after my relationship with Sam melted away. I trusted Ben. I knew that we had a lot in common. We had known each other for many years.

The next few weeks, I spent in heaven: I would see him again.

And when I wasn't in heaven, I was in hell: I would see him again and I had no idea what would happen.

He arrived on a Saturday in May, and Barcelona welcomed him with chilly winter weather. I saw him from a distance when he left the security area. He hadn't changed at all, maybe just some stray grays in his hair, as tall as always, his walk a bit gawky, as if he didn't know what to do with his tall body. I had worried about how it would be for someone as small as me to hug a man of 6 feet 4 inches. It turned out to be easy. When he saw me, he said, "You're taller than I remembered." I smiled; we seemed to have had the same preoccupation.

The next morning, I woke up on my sofa while he slept in my bedroom. While I moved around, I saw how he secretly observed my movements. I smiled and kept my distance. I felt that he was interested in me, but I wanted to allow myself the time I needed. The following days passed easily. We walked through the city, and I showed him my new home. Ben was gentle and respectful, just as always. Always gentlemanly, he opened doors for me. We talked about our relationships and our lives. He played with my cats. I felt light and easy. We talked about his kids, and he showed me photos of his home in Denver.

Three days later, we hired a rental car and went to Tamariu at the Costa Brava. It was a wonderful little village in a small cove surrounded by rugged pine-covered cliffs. The houses of the village shimmered snow-white in the afternoon sun. We went to the main hotel, which had huge balconies and was directly on the beach, and asked for a room. I decided to book a double room with him because I trusted that he would respect me, and I also trusted that he would never play games with me.

When we entered the room, he suddenly and gently kissed my forehead. I didn't react. We went to the beach together and went out for dinner. Later, we watched a German detective series in bed and went to sleep.

The next morning, we were woken by the sun, which shone brightly into our room. We had breakfast and then went to the beach. While lying there, Ben started to massage my back. His hands were warm and soft, and he did it lovingly. In the afternoon, while at another beach—a wonderful cove with pine trees and crystal clear blue-green water—I returned his caresses. Later, we went for a short walk up a cliff, he helping me to climb the stones, and then we went out for dinner. At night, we stayed in our room and watched another movie. This time, Ben invited me to lie next to him, and he held me in his arms while we watched the movie. When the movie was over, he tenderly pulled me on top of him. We were stroking each other. I knew that it was time to kiss him. I knew that I was afraid of it. I looked into his eyes and said, "I'm afraid of this."

Ben replied quietly, "I'm afraid, too." After a while, we kissed each other. Nothing more. Just kissed each other. I had managed it like any other person. I was perfectly able to control all my inner parts and just enjoy the kissing. Nothing else happened. Later, we fell asleep while holding each other tightly.

The following days were a dream. We lay together at the beach, he gently massaging me. We walked through the city holding hands. And six days after his arrival, I had sex with him and I managed to open up and surrender. I knew that I had deeply fallen in love with him.

That night, I had a brief attack of fear when we stood at Port Vell at night. In the sky, a huge full moon was shining. Ben sat down to have a cigar. I took a puff and was hit by my fear that the relationship would be a repeat of what had happened with Sam. An unbearable pressure struck my breast. Had I created the same experience once more? A man who was unreachable? Would Ben go home to Denver and never show up again? Agony entered my heart. I needed to be alone for a while.

I looked at Ben and asked him whether he would return to my apartment alone. He looked back, astonished, and said that he did not want to but he would do it. I gave him my keys and nodded. I started walking. With each step I took, I felt that it was the wrong path. After 50 feet, I turned around and returned. I looked into his eyes and said, "I'm sorry."

He looked at me, smiled, and said, "Lovely that you are back." Then he took my hand and said, "I will never let you go again." It was the most beautiful sentence I had ever heard in my life. We walked away from the port in the direction of my apartment, side by side, holding hands.

Sunday was Ben's last day in Barcelona, and we walked down the Passeig Maritim in Barceloneta. In the distance was Port Olimpic, with its white sailing boats, and before that, the famous bronze fish statue with the two tower blocks. Below that, at street level, were stylish beach restaurants and palm trees, which stood up high against the blue sky. People sat on the strand in swimsuits, enjoying the sun. Some tourists had already caught too many rays. Others had a drink in one of the *chiringuitos*, the little bars on the beach. Walking hand in hand with Ben, a touch of sadness hit me. His visit had clarified where I stood. I had fallen in love and I had told him so. Now we would separate; our future was uncertain.

I looked into his eyes and said, "I have shown you who I am. I can't give you more."

He bent down and gave me a kiss on my forehead.

We went to the pier at Port Olimpic and took a photo together, sitting on the pier and holding each other tightly. Never before had I allowed a man to know me so intimately, to be so close to me.

The next day, Ben left my apartment in the early morning. Later that day, he texted me that he had arrived home safely. My week with Ben had been the most wonderful time I had shared with a man in my life so far. It felt like a happy dance, light and harmonious. I felt sure that everything would work out fine. And the first two weeks did work out fine.

During a phone call some days later, Ben said, "The worst thing that could happen to me right now would be to lose you."

This sentence gave me so much confidence and made me so happy. "Don't worry, I'll call you if I get fearful and want to run away. I know how to manage myself now." I never wanted to lose him. "You are a wonderful man."

"You are a wonderful woman."

It sounded honest.

Two weeks later, I woke up at 3:00 a.m. Suddenly, I was fully awake. My inner voice told me to check my email. There was a message from Ben. He told me that he had a lot of work to do and that one of his twin daughters had been in the hospital because she had broken her arm. It was written in a nice, cheerful tone, and he ended by saying, "It would be nice if we saw each other again and also nice if we never met again." Was Ben really saying this to me?!

Ben's words hit me so hard that I lost connection with my wise part. I should have withdrawn and just waited to see what would happen. I felt so much for him that I couldn't.

I read the email again. Maybe I had not understood the email. I tried to phone him. I knew that I was projecting all my experience with Sam on to him, and I wanted to make sure I understood what he really meant. No answer. I looked at the message again. All I understood was that he had told me in a quiet way that there was no place for me in his life. I had never expected this from him. He had known me for such a long time. Could he really think that I had just been having casual fun? He knew that I had fallen in love with him. I couldn't reach him, so I replied by email and did exactly the wrong thing. I told him that I wanted a relationship with him and that we could find a way to create a good relationship. The next day, he wrote me that I was overreacting.

For the next few days, he was suddenly unavailable by phone, made promises to call me, and never did. For a few days, I was so confused by what had happened that I became clingy. I wanted to understand what was happening on the other side of the ocean. There was never an answer. I was in a tunnel, trying to find my way in complete darkness. Why had I been so stupid as to invite him to Barcelona? Why had I thought that he was different from other men? Even worse, why had I trusted him and opened my heart to him? I was angry with him and even more angry with myself. I knew that it was difficult for me to enter relationships. And I had been afraid that he would abandon me without an honest explanation, the way Sam had.

A week later, Ben wrote me a second message: "Natalie, I am just coming out of a relationship. I do not know whether I want to have a new relationship . . . You have to understand. It was the first time in a long time that I had to make a decision without my partner. It had nothing to do with you."

Nothing to do with me? For me, the way he had treated me during the past week had everything to do with me.

His message was full of panic, just like many messages I had received from Sam. I had to let him go. It did not matter how important he was to me. I asked myself what action would give me strength right now. I decided to write him back: "I am really hurt by the way you treated me. I understand your situation, but if you aren't clear with me and if you're not doing what you're saying, then you're not treating me well. I would have wished that you had the courage to phone me and talk about it. I have not deserved to be treated like this, least of all by you. I have trusted you. And what hurts me most is that I have the impression that you just came here to get a bit of sex after your separation."

My reaction wasn't the wisest one. I should have said, "I see that you are not yet ready for a relationship"—but I needed to express my feelings. Ben and I were connected by fourteen years of friendship. I would have been able to deal with a clear *No, I don't want a relationship with you*, but his disappearing without calling me and allowing me to hear his voice hurt me.

When I had experienced that short attack of fear at the harbor, Ben had told me, "Things never turn out as badly as you fear." Actually, what had happened was that my biggest nightmare had hit me without warning. Maybe he would overcome his fears and phone me within a couple of weeks to explain what had happened. I would feel better if I knew the truth. But I couldn't do anything. It was his step to take. I couldn't control him.

For the next four weeks, I did everything kind for myself and focused on my business. I did my full program for lovesickness: flower essences, visualizations, prayer, and Reiki, not to mention calling my friends, crying, and going through all the stages of sadness and anger. Each morning, I asked myself what would be the kindest thing for me to do for myself and I did it. I took good care of my inner child, who had been traumatized by the abrupt ending. She felt dirty again, used and thrown away. My dignity was hurt again. I knew that my feelings were produced by my past and I managed them. I knew that part of my hurt was due to the fact that Ben hadn't been clear with me; he hadn't been able to phone me to tell me the truth. I had lost a lover, and I had lost a very good friend. I couldn't change this fact.

After four weeks, I stopped doubting myself. I had observed him and I had allowed myself time. This time, I had done it well. I wasn't perfect. For me, having sex with a man was more than just fun. It always will be. It had taken me more than eleven years to learn to surrender in making love to a man, to have sex without feeling like a prostitute. That was part of my story and I had healed it. He didn't know that. He couldn't know that.

For him, sexuality was fun and a diversion. He had come out of a twenty-one-year relationship. He had never before gone through the mourning process after a relationship. It was his first time. He had not yet let go of his past. He had never in his adult life stayed alone. He had never in his adult life decided anything without his partner. I had always decided alone. He had four kids. He just wasn't ready for a new relationship. He didn't know what a healthy relationship was. For him, a new relationship would be yet another change in his life. He was afraid to start something new.

Ben had his journey and I had mine. It had not been the right time for him—nor was he the right partner for me. I wanted somebody who was honest, who had courage, and who had healed his past. Despite the pain, the breakup with Ben was a positive thing in that it helped me to connect even more closely with myself. I just trusted that the relationship had happened for a reason and that ultimately, it would be for my highest good—and that one day I would understand.

A few weeks later, I flew to India and presented my workshop on storytelling. After two weeks, I was on my way back from Kochi to Bangalore and spent a night in the jungle. I sat on the balcony of a beautiful lodge in the jungle of Kerala, India, and listened to the *chirr* of millions of crickets. It was an amazing concert that was so loud that it drowned out the burbling of the little river that crossed the area a few yards away from my balcony. Once in a while, there was a cracking sound of an animal I didn't know.

I sat in the shimmering light of a candle and looked at the green leaves of the bushes in the jungle.

In my training for the Indian counselors, I had told them. "Each story has its beauty. We just need to be able to recognize it."

The beauty of my story with Ben was that I had opened my heart for love again and that I had dared to take a risk. I had had the courage to jump. I had shown him the real me without a mask. I was proud that I had tried. He had meant so much to me that I would have regretted it all my life if I hadn't tried. Finally, I had accepted that I couldn't control what happened in him and I had decided to do what was best for me and what gave me strength. I was now the most important person in my life; I had reclaimed my power.

I knew that I was well prepared to have a healthy and harmonious relationship and that I would always let go of relationships that weren't good for me. The relationship I desired would happen at the right time and in the right place.

At that moment, a loving voice in my head sang my own personal credo, which I had written down and always carried in my handbag:

My future is a cheerful dance in blue.

If the gods were to give me advice, they would say, *Don't worry*.

If my guardian angel had a message of hope, he would say, *All is well*.

And so it is.

My Magical Story

Creating a story about my future gave me the strength to embrace my shadow and heal my past. It also gave me the persistence and inspiration I needed to move forward with my life. After the death of my mother, I read some books by Elisabeth Kübler-Ross, a psychiatrist and a pioneer in near-death studies, to get a better understanding about death and to find the meaning of life. I started to think about my own death and what I wanted to happen in my life. I decided that I wanted to be able to die peacefully and to tell a powerful and inspiring story on the day I died, and that I want to have found true love. After all, what's important is not how I entered this world but how I leave it. And I knew that it was up to me to create a life worth living. I believe that everyone who has experienced a difficult childhood has the power to create an especially beautiful future. And I see my creation of a wonderful future as the most loving thing I can do for myself. Based on the stories of my past and of my imagined future, I created my magical story, which continuously evolves and which shows me the way to the future that I want.

It was a warm day in spring when a kitten was born. She had dark brown eyes and was the youngest of the family. One year later, her mother, an elegant gazelle with slender and fragile legs, fell in love with a gruff German shepherd, whose quick temper changed from one minute to the next, like a sunny summer day that turns stormy. The gazelle left the kitten's father to live with the German shepherd, and the kitten moved with them into a dark, fog-filled cave. Sometimes there were explosions with cold red flashes, which frightened her.

A little later, the kitten experienced sexual violence, which shocked her soul. She withdrew into a castle with glass walls, which were higher than Mount Everest and wider than the Amazon rainforest. The walls protected her so that she would not feel the pain. The gazelle did all she could to care for her kitten, although she herself was fighting death. One day, she lost the fight, and the angels protected the kitten and showed her the way out of the dark cave.

The kitten became a cat, and the castle turned into a glass prison. She fell in love with a huge brown bear but left him because she had to find her wings to be able to fly. The moon guided her on her way, and she found a village full of light and love, far away from her land. The Universe sent her a wonderful violet fairy with black hair who radiated love and tenderness. Thanks to her help, the cat was able to break the glass walls into pieces. Behind them, she found the innocent kitten, full of love and joy. That day, the cat found her wings. And from that day forward, she was able to fly and to protect the kitten from all harm.

The cat fell in love with a wolf, a good and trusted friend, who was important to her. It seemed as though they might live together happily, but she had to let him go, even though her heart nearly burst. Thanks to this experience, she acquired her two most precious jewels: her healed heart and her power.

Infused with the magical energy of India, the cat transformed herself into a wise Sphinx with loving power, and she told her stories to heal other animals. A little later, she visited a wonderful green city on another continent; the city was surrounded by magical mountains and forests full of fairies. While she sat by the sea and watched its amazing beauty, two whales whispered from a distance, "My dear cat, it is time to leave your village. You need the green of nature and the breeze of the sea. You

have to venture into the world and build your new home here."
A miracle happened and a few months later she lived in this
wonderful green place.

On a warm day in March, a mermaid sent her a majestic and
wise lion, who loved her with all his heart, and she loved him.
They created a relationship full of love and light. Then the Universe gave the Sphinx and the lion the greatest gift of all: a kitten. The Sphinx enjoyed each moment with her family, and she
loved to lean against the lion's shoulder and feel his fur. She continued to write and teach, and her stories helped many animals
to heal their hearts and find true love. Many times, she went to
India to share her stories and her wisdom. Each time, her life
acquired even more colors.

On the day she turned 110, she knew that it was time to go.
She said good-bye to her dear friends, her beloved animals,
and her cherished family and thanked them for their journey
together. She went down to the sea with the lion, and they sat by
the beach in the light of the moon. After a while, she gave him a
final kiss and a long embrace. The lion watched her as she went
into the sea and disappeared into the waves with a smile on her
face, accompanied on her last journey by her friends, the two
whales. When he returned home, the house was filled with the
joy, laughter, and dancing of her friends, who celebrated her life.
They said, "Her life was a cheerful dance in blue."

And on special nights, when the full moon is really bright,
you can still hear her stories in the murmur of the sea.

My magical story gives my past a good place in my heart, and
it infuses me with hope for and faith in my future. My past and
my future work together: if I have accepted my past as it was
and if I can look at it in peace, a happy future can arrive.

Especially for You

At the end of my August 2013 two-day workshop in Bangalore, India, I asked the group of counselors what they had learned during the training. A young Indian woman in a blue dress with golden ornaments, long, dark hair, and brilliant brown eyes said in a firm voice, "I have learned in this workshop that if I heal myself, I can better heal my clients." In that moment, I smiled because I had transmitted to the counselors the message I wanted to share. The more healing a therapist has done, the better she can support her clients in their own processes.

I took a long time to start my inner work to heal myself because I had negative beliefs about therapists, I lacked self-esteem, and I was unable to ask for help. When I finally started my inner work, the changes happened rapidly, and I became aware of my immense self-healing capacity. Here is what I did to heal myself:

- I created a loving relationship with myself.
  I learned to love and respect myself. In this way, I developed a healthy self-esteem, which is vital to a healthy relationship. Loving myself is an inner process. It allows me to be authentic and speak my truth, to leave a relationship that violates my boundaries, and to enjoy life as a single person until the intimate love relationship arrives.
- I became a complete person.
  When I healed my childhood wounds and other

negative experiences of my past, I became whole.
I learned to be aware of my needs and found out
that I can give myself what I need. This means that
I am independent and can consciously choose the
relationships that I want to have.

- I learned about new realities.
As a child, my reality was shaped by abusive
relationships. I didn't know anything different, and
I thought that all relationships were struggle and
suffering. As an adult, I learned that there are other
realities. Healthy relationships do exist and creating
them isn't a mystery. Behaviors and attitudes that
nourish a positive, joyful relationship can be learned.

- I connected with my dreams.
When I allowed myself to believe in my dreams and to
follow them, this gave me the power and the motivation
to heal myself.

It takes two people to create a relationship. One day, I will meet
the right partner and realize my dreams. Meanwhile, I will let
go of relationships that do not match my dreams. And all the
while, I will enjoy my life and follow my dreams.

If I can do this, you can, too. I hope that this book has encour-
aged you to start your journey today.

As special thanks for buying my book, you can download the following free resources from my webpage www.nataliejovanic.com.
Claim your free gift and experience the magic of story, freedom
and love today!

FREE REPORT

12 Secrets to Attract a Healthy Relationship

Here are some of the things you will find in this report:
- You'll learn the twelve most common mistakes that can happen on the journey to a healthy relationship and how you can turn them around.
- You'll discover the unconscious obstacles that might be holding you back from having the relationship you want.
- You'll find out how to become the confident person you are meant to be and how to attract great relationships like a magnet.

Just go to the website www.nataliejovanic.com/12-secrets/ and download the free report today!

7 Magical Principles for a Loving Relationship With Yourself

Change starts with yourself. You are the most important person in your life. A loving and healthy relationship with yourself gives you positive energy and joy, and it improves your relationships with other people. This report helps you to connect with yourself. Here are some of the details of this report:

- You'll learn about seven magical principles that will remake your relationship with yourself.
- You'll discover twenty-four easy, inspirational activities that will improve your relationship with yourself.
- You'll be empowered to become a radiant star, giving you the ability to choose relationships that serve you well.

Start today to transform your life! Go to www.nataliejovanic. com/7magicalprinciples/ and download this free report today!

Bibliography of Further Reading

Following are books that have been very helpful to me and may be useful to you.

Bloom, Lisa. *Cinderella and the Coach: The Power of Storytelling for Coaching Success*. [Zikhron Ya'akov, Israel]: Lisa Bloom, 2011.

Castanyer, Olga. *La asertividad: Expresión de una sana autoestima* [Assertiveness: Expression of a Healthy Self-Esteem]. Bilbao, Spain: Editorial Desclée de Brouwer, S.A., 2004.

Hendrix, Harville. *Keeping the Love You Find: A Single Person's Guide to Achieving Lasting Love*. London: Simon & Schuster UK Ltd, 1995.

Kritsberg, Wayne. *Die unsichtbare Wunde: Sexueller Missbrauch in der Kindheit—Das Trauma erkennen und ueberwinden* [The Invisible Wound: A New Approach to Healing Childhood Sexual Abuse]. Zurich: Oesch Verlag AG, 1993.

Kübler-Ross, Elisabeth. *On Death and Dying*. New York: Scribner, 1997. First published 1969 by Macmillan.

———. *Death: The Final Stage of Growth*. New York: Simon and Schuster / Touchstone, 1986. First published 1975 by Prentice-Hall

Myers, Linda Joy. *The Power of Memoir: How to Write Your Healing Story*. San Francisco: Jossey-Bass, 2010.

Naparstek, Belleruth. *Your Sixth Sense: Unlocking the Power of Your Intuition*. New York: HaperCollins Publishers, 1997.

Noguchi, Yoshinori. *La ley del espejo: Una regla mágica que da solución a cualquier problema en la vida* [The Law of the Mirror: A Magic Rule to Solve Any Problem in Life]. Barcelona: Comanegra, 2009.

Orloff, Judith, M.D. *Emotional Freedom: Liberate Yourself from Negative Emotions and Transform Your Life*. New York: Crown Publishing Group, 2009.

Paul, Margaret, and Erika J. Chopich. *Das Arbeitsbuch zur Aussoehnung mit dem Inneren Kind* [The Workbook for Reconciliation with the Inner Child]. Berlin: Ullstein Taschenbuch, 2005.

Riso, Walter. *Los límites del amor: Como amar sin renunciar a ti mismo* [The Limits of Love: How to Love Without Giving Up Yourself]. Barcelona: Editorial Planeta, 2009.

Schaefer, Thomas. *Was die Seele krank macht und was sie heilt: Die psychotherapeutische Arbeit von Bert Hellinger* [What Makes the Soul Ill and What It Heals: The Psychotherapeutic Work of Bert Hellinger]. Munich: Droemersche Verlagsanstalt Th. Knaur Nachf., 1997.

Schram, Peninnah, and Rachayl Eckstein Davis. *The Apple Tree's Discovery*. Illustrated by Wendy W. Lee. Minneapolis, MN: Kar-Ben Publishing, 2012.

Shoshanna, Brenda. *Zen and the Art of Falling in Love*. New York: Simon & Schuster Paperbacks, 2003.

Thoele, Sue Patton. *El coraje de ser tu misma: Una guía para superar tu dependencia emocional y crecer interiormente* [The Courage to Be Yourself: A Woman's Guide to Emotional Strength and Self-Esteem]. Madrid: Editorial EDAF, 2011.

Acknowledgments

My achievements would not have been possible without the help and support of my wonderful friends, who live all over the world. I thank them for caring for me, accepting me, and appreciating me; for believing in me in the moments when I didn't; for seeing my light when I saw darkness; for trusting me and for loving and accepting me as I was; for helping me grow and supporting me in following my dreams; and for giving me a new form of family—a family of souls.

My special thanks go to Amei for our mutual journey of twenty-two years; for the hikes, the laughter, the tears, and the dreams we've shared together. I also owe particular gratitude to Sabine for being the pioneer in her exploration of spirituality; she gave me the example I needed so that I dared to follow my own inner knowing and connect with this invisible world.

Profound respect and appreciation go to Olga of the association Street Heroes of India for her encouraging words. I am much obliged to my dear friend and spiritual teacher Margarita Alonso; her channeled advice from the Universe gave me the courage to finally write this book. Many thanks to my friend Maria_T. Febreiro for reading my second draft and giving me her loving critique.

I am deeply grateful for the wonderful Story-Coaching work by Lisa Bloom, who introduced me to the magical world of storytelling and who helped me express the scenes of my life that had been hidden in my soul. I extend my sincere thanks to the Center for Right Relationships (CRR Global) for its Organization and Relationship Systems Coaching curriculum, which has an inspirational perspective on relationships and how to make them work. The curriculum gave me the hope and trusting outlook on relationships that I had been searching for. My wonderful teachers from beth-constelaciones in Barcelona, Sylvia Kabelka and

Ángela Aparicio, have my everlasting gratitude for their support and wisdom. I am beholden to my friend Ferran Moreno for his exceptional work in healing my body from sexual violence.

Many thanks to my copy editor, Kathy Kaiser, for her thoughtfulness, accuracy, understanding, and patience in her work to make the best of my story.

Finally, I thank my ex-partners for being in relationship with me. Each of you helped me to move forward in my life—to connect more with myself and to heal a bit more. I am grateful for our time together, and I will keep you in my heart always.

About the Author

Natalie Jovanic is a relationship expert, systemic coach, and author.

Her clients are mainly successful professionals who experience difficulty or pain in their relationships and who want to connect with their essence and have healthy relationships. With her help, clients activate their self-healing capacities, connect with their inner resources and explore their needs. They connect with their inner voice and their soul. As a result, they heal their hearts and follow their dreams. They experience more hope, inner peace, and satisfaction, and they are empowered to create the relationships they dream of, with themselves and with others.

Natalie Jovanic also presents workshops on storytelling for counselors, therapists, and coaches, in which she and participants explore how the magic of storytelling can heal trauma and violence. Find out more about her work at www.nataliejovanic.com.